Advance Praise

"Uplifting, inspiring, and hilarious... Mix in a sprinkle of heartbreak and a whole lot of wisdom, and you have *How to Survive a Breakup*. Lisa Cleary is an exciting new voice well worth listening to."

> — Richard Chizmar, *New York Times* best-selling author, *Gwendy's Button Box*, *Gwendy's Magic Feather* and *The Girl on the Porch*

"*How to Survive a Breakup* is a heartwarming, helpful, and humorous guide to the intricacies of navigating a breakup at an age when many have settled down. We all know that there is so much more to breaking up than a broken heart, and so many couples stay together perhaps longer than they should out of emotional or financial convenience. Lisa Cleary provides a refreshing and honest voice, along with practical advice. I could not only identify with her story, full of her signature wit and grace, but found her advice both helpful and practical—even as a happily married woman (and one without children), I now have a handy checklist of what to do if I ever need to break a lease suddenly one day. Kudos to Lisa for having the courage, humor, and wisdom to share her journey with us!"

— Amelia Cotter, author, poet, and storyteller; author of *This House: The True Story of a Girl and a Ghost, Maryland Ghosts: Paranormal Encounters in the Free State*, and the children's book *Breakfast with Bigfoot*

HOW TO SURVIVE A BREAKUP

HOW TO SURVIVE A BREAKUP

(When all of your friends are birthing their second child)

LISA CLEARY

Apprentice House Press
Loyola University Maryland

First Edition

Hardcover ISBN: 978-1-62720-265-7
Paperback ISBN: 978-1-62720-266-4
Ebook ISBN: 978-1-62720-267-1

Printed in the United States of America

Acquisitions & Editing: Isabella DePalma
Design: Apprentice House Press
Promotion plan: Isabella DePalma

Published by Apprentice House Press

Apprentice House Press
Loyola University Maryland
4501 N. Charles Street
Baltimore, MD 21210
410.617.5265
www.ApprenticeHouse.com
info@ApprenticeHouse.com

To my mom, dad, brothers, sister, and nephew;
and to Theodore, Missy, Hobson, and Riley.

And, to every person who has encouraged me to
trust and let go to God's plan.

1

Are You a Type A, Anxious Overachiever... Too?

So, you're almost 30 years old.

The age when those "30-by-30" lists come into play and life markers become actual achievements. When you can repeat the four Cs of diamonds in your sleep, and the stages of an unborn baby become synonymous with fruit. When you realize that PMI and HOAs aren't STDs; they're financial annoyances…

And then, well, there's me.

The late bloomer. The socially stunted. The individual who isn't sure if her life is the consequence of bad decisions or the culmination of bad luck. I say this because, two years ago, I experienced The Summer Slap-Down: a mass layoff, a tumultuous break up after a rather long-term relationship, the subsequent start of a new job, and two unexpected moves—simultaneously, in a matter of three neat months.

What's the funniest part of it all?

Well, I'm a writer. And, in fact, I'm a health and happiness-based writer. I'm the type of person who writes those kinds of lists, like: "What kind of friend are you?" Answer: "Just read this list and look inside of your pantry: you're nutty and smooth like peanut butter, or boring like whole grain bread and everyone's forced to be with you."

Suffice to say, the irony was real: my own advice had not worked for me. But I do stand overqualified for having experienced many of life's major stressors in a compressed amount of time. There's a special sort of feeling for when you're packing up your desk, wondering, *How am I going to support myself, and can I justify my unemployment funds to cover my weekly allowance of wine?* And then, when you go home to your apartment to pack up the rest of your life, you're left to wonder, *What am I going to do with the rest of my life?*

Where am I going to live?

That summer, I cried for maybe the fifth time ever.

But I Planned My Life Out... In My Planner

I have always been a Type A, anxious overachiever, and therefore a planner by default. That mindset is my greatest attribute and, yet, my fatal flaw. To this day, I map out weekly goals that translate to long-term achievements, color code them as I go, and then evaluate my accomplishments at the end of the week. It's both exhausting and highly effective.

So when, at 31 years old, I had not been able to show off an engagement, a well furnished home, and an established career as a novelist, I questioned why—and how—all of my planning had gone awry. I wasn't even in the process of building up to those goals. I was breaking up, moving out, and stomping on life.

Indulging in my melodramatics, I kept asking myself: why were others married and birthing their second child, when I was just starting over in almost every facet of my life? I realized that there were worse injustices in life and that shitty things in life happen, but I still felt compelled to compete with everyone else. That's what happens when you're Type A. The thing was, though, my perspective was off-kilter at the time, because I felt like I had nothing to compete with. I felt like I had nothing to show for myself.

That summer, friends quickly noticed my significant decline on social media and lack of HCPs[1*]. I ceased posting artfully plated, home-cooked meals for two. I stopped sharing uplifting quotes from literature, because no one should care about selfless love anymore. It didn't exist. And, after I got laid off, I never again mentioned how cool it was to partake in yoga at lunch and to be part of an elite group of writers. (Who needs a proper salary when you can get paid in free Starbucks?) No one wanted to see what I was really doing in between my recurring meltdowns, which consisted of scouring Match.com profiles, wondering what <u>bottom of the barrel</u> was left for me. No one knew that

1* Happy Couple Photos

I'd eat a heavy dinner, so I could try to fall asleep by 8 p.m., with my now ex-boyfriend in the other room of our apartment, packing to move out.

Most especially, no one wanted to hear me whine and worry anymore. I had exhausted all sympathetic outlets.

Even though I felt like I had failed in not hitting the main life markers that so many of my friends had already accomplished, I wasn't overly worried about the success of my career or my personal finances. I was still in control of my journey as a writer, even when taking layoffs into account, because I largely only needed to rely on myself to get the job done. My main concern, however, was the one facet of my life that required the willing compliance of one other person: a relationship.

I Feel Juvenile

Trusting life's plan, particularly with regard to love and relationships, was a daunting task when reality plagued my own family and friends. Divorces and child custody hearings? I don't know how they did it. Abusive relationships? I'm awed at the courage it took to walk away. Sudden deaths of spouses? It's a pain I don't know how my loved ones carry to this day.

My breakup seemed trivial in comparison to the aches and pains of others, but it still hurt. I hurt. I had loved someone whole-heartedly for many years, and I felt conned and empty. I wondered what my ultimate life plan was and what obstacles I still needed to jump.

The thought of not being able to fully control my future was frightening, and I no longer wondered when I'd have the chance at legitimate love; I wondered if.

Breakups near, during, and beyond your thirties make for incredibly lonely and isolating times. A breakup is nowhere near as jolting as the "D" word: "divorce," which is why many family and friends may even fail to acknowledge the situation at hand. Still, the sting of it all lingers. Breakups are also a far cry from ones in your twenties, a time when your best girlfriends could blow off shifts and take sick days to be by your bedside with no questions asked.

Now, because friends have increasing priorities, like significant others, husbands and families, more demanding positions at work, and even worries over aging parents, the sympathetic shoulders to cry on are harder to come by. People are busy. When I juxtaposed my voids against the happiness of my mostly female friends, many of whom were married and even pregnant with their second child, it made me want to push them even further away. I didn't want to break down to my best friend about my fear of loneliness when her child was screaming, ready for a feeding, in the background.

I felt so… incredibly juvenile.

During the course of the next year, as I adjusted to a new apartment and a new job, I felt very alone. I had never lived alone, and so moving into unfamiliar surroundings, by myself, was frightening and I became depressed. No one prepares you for what it feels like to move out of a very luxe rented apartment, afforded by two salaries, to the cheapest unit in the basement of a complex that's thirty miles outside of the city.

And so, I barely cried, and I mostly mulled. The holidays were anxious times for me, with the early darkness of late fall and winter particularly tough. At the New Year, I congratulated a burst of friends on their engagements, some of whom I thought would never settle down, and some of whom had moved past their first marriage and were now planning for their second. Come Valentine's Day, I ordered cheesy breadsticks and broccoli bites and watched *Gone Girl*. And, as a new spring approached, I realized that I was really alone.

Please RSVP to Help Me

Even though I knew it was detrimental, I continued to compare my life to everyone's social media posts: more bachelorette parties. More baby showers. Too many festivities. I wondered why Bed, Bath & Beyond didn't encourage single people like myself to open up registries as a declared rite of passage: if you're 30 years old and single, you have more than earned the right to throw yourself a party and invite all of your friends to buy you expensive things.

However, no one helped me to expand upon my own homeware. I instead racked up my credit card to purchase what had been split up and taken during the move. I saved my Domino's preference settings in my phone, so that ordering pizza could be swiftly completed with several taps. I buried myself under my comforter whenever I felt full, and slept in past noon on the weekends. My planning and long-term goals were no more.

I was feeling really sorry for myself.

I'm Here: Because Everyone Else is Busy

Now, I understand what it feels like to hurt, but then to stand back up to whatever life throws at you. I understand what it feels like to achingly assume that you're five steps behind your friends, and how it feels when you can't afford your own summer vacation, because you've been invited to your sixth wedding of the season... without a guest. I understand your "Duo by Default" fear, and how it feels to be the thirteenth wheel at a dinner outing that you planned. Now, I understand that this is life and that, no matter how much you have, you'll never be happy if you expect everything to be perfect all of the time.

Finally, I know now what it takes to heal and what expectations you should set for yourself through the journey. Happiness is work. In fact, it's some damn hard work, and the really tough mental kind, like my days of high school AP statistics, when I had three tutors and still almost failed.

And that's why I'm here. I'm not famous, and I'm not a life coach. I'm not going to jumpstart your magical life transformation to set you on a new path in just 48 hours. I'm here as a writer who used to dole out lists and advice to now share how I realistically recovered from my breakup. I'm here to stop you from buying Puffs lotion tissues in bulk and to push you to climb out from underneath of your covers.

So what if you're 30 years old? Or, over the age of 30, like me? I'm here to show you how, day by day, everything will be OK. I'm here to talk to the women and men who feel like they have no one to talk to, because everyone else is busy.

It's time to get real together—and, let me start by sharing my story.

2

There's Always a Story

Before we dig deeper, let me share my story. Everyone always has a story.

I was an unsure late bloomer when it came to relationships, and I always second guessed myself. In high school, I never felt confident about my appearance and finger-painted my face with greasy drugstore makeup, and I was the geeky, behind-the-scenes writer of the newspaper and yearbook committees. I never got asked on dates and always went to homecoming dances with friends or by myself. I was desperate to be liked, but I never felt worthy of it.

Fast forward to my collegiate days: I entered college as a 17-year-old virgin and was teased relentlessly for it. "No, Leah, I have never seen a penis," or "But I'm scared of STDs, and he's wearing salmon shorts," were the frequent answers I repeated. Over and over again.

I still cared what others had to say, but this time I wasn't going to play desperate: I promised myself going into college that I would lose my virginity to my first love and, eventually, I did. It was the perfect day, and our relationship went on to last for about four years.

But, like with many college couples, we broke up about a year after we graduated, and so I threw myself into my career. I was already working full time in medical editing and publishing, a job which largely required me to thumb through page proofs after page proofs of vividly depicted genital infections. After a year of that, I also enrolled in graduate school—full time. I kept at the grueling schedule of work from 9 a.m. to 5 p.m., classes from 6 p.m. to 9 p.m., and assignments from 10 p.m. until well past 2 a.m. While I'm a naturally driven person, my motivation was based off of one factor: I was desperate for some sort of passion in my life. I needed a drastic change.

On top of all of that—a few months after I started graduate school—an opportunity to work part time for NBC as a daily health columnist was offered, and I jumped at the chance, knowing that the exposure could open many doors. I wrote early in the mornings and late at night, after my classes and assignments, and I worked even longer hours during the weekends.

I maybe slept four hours a night and managed the best that I could. Every Sunday evening, I meal planned: I ordered a week's worth of takeout at Wendy's at once and, for the rest of the week, I dined on containers of chili, hamburger patties, and cold, soggy fries. I took naps in my car during lunch breaks, and I was frantic but organized. During that period and, most important of all, I only had time to focus on one thing: myself. I quickly became self-aware of my capabilities as a writer, and my confidence flourished.

That mindset soon began to permeate the rest of my life.

Over the course of the next two years, I dated off and on, for periods of six months or so at a time, and no one ever seemed to stick. If the chemistry wasn't there, I moved on. Instead of spending time on mediocre date after date, I finally acknowledged that I had the power to control my own dating life and denied easy, available opportunities to free myself up for more substantial individuals—a direction that I had been traveling all along in my writing career. Not only was I redirecting my mindset in all aspects of my life, but I was finally taking control of it.

Of course, along with this revelation, I also came to disdainfully realize that dating is a roller coaster of hopeful expectations and realistic disappointments. Countless first dates were last dates. On one date, a guy proceeded to text and take calls throughout dinner. When the date was over and he dropped me off, I was surprised by his quick sleight of hand, which happened to find its way to my left boob for an uninvited tug.

I even exhausted my favorite spot at meeting men, which was a little Mediterranean restaurant that seated twenty, located down the street from my apartment. I loved their pumpkin hummus and their spiced sauces drizzled over quinoa, but I had to stop going after the cook commented on seeing me all of the time "but with different men."

Then, when I was 28 years old, I met Mark.

He was exactly what I needed: a trustworthy, genuine source of comfort. We shared mutual friends, and so I felt safe with him. He seemed motivated with a competitive job in business management and well educated with his MBA.

By that time, I had also completed graduate school and my contract with NBC had ended. I was explosive—I needed to experience a proper social life, and Mark happened to be quite the socialite. We became inseparable over trivia nights and cocktail specials, and he showed me the corner bars that looked like dives but were really among the area's top-rated restaurants. We spilled secrets over happy hours and drank until the bars closed, and even then we were invited to stay after hours. We broke out into slow, romantic dances in public whenever we felt like it, and we were fun and intoxicating. Mark and I made so many friends. We just drew people in.

Never one to be impulsively led by my emotions, I was surprised when I found myself madly in love with Mark. He developed into someone who was more than just fun. He listened and cared about my insecurities and fears, and I could openly vent to him about anything. He always responded that my personal issues were ones we'd work on together as a team, and he always said "thank you" whenever I kissed him good night on the cheek. Mark was a WYSIWYG type of guy—you know, the What You See Is What You Get—which to me was an attribute, because he was comfortable with being himself and by being honest. I couldn't have asked for more.

From a career standpoint, I had been planning on moving to Washington, DC, before I had even met Mark. Right when we had begun dating, I had ecstatically quit my old job and was beginning a new one at a startup in DC—it was the next self-proclaimed big chapter of my career. I had been in the midst of scouting out neighborhoods, but I listened to my instincts and paused the hunt, because coming home to Mark offered me more of a promising future than even my career at that time. For that year, I commuted back and forth from Baltimore to DC, three hours a day on top of ten-hour days. I saw Mark as an investment worthy of prioritizing.

Unfortunately, I wish I had listened when my instincts flagged the bad parts of him, too. Like with my bed, for instance. The bed I was using at the time was handed down to me by my grandparents, and it was a queen-size wooden frame with a thick footboard. During the first month or two of dating, Mark and I spent almost every day together. He slept over as many nights as I slept over his house, and he made out just fine in my bed. It was a compromise, as any relationship should be. It certainly was easier on my schedule whenever he slept over my apartment, because I came home relatively late, near 8:30 p.m.—unlike Mark, who was home by 4:00 p.m. and able to run errands, go to the gym, and eat dinner before I even made it back. On the nights we stayed at my apartment, I could simultaneously do laundry and other little things, like take out the trash.

On the nights I stayed over his house, however, my schedule was even more cumbersome. I needed to pit-stop at my apartment to eat dinner, get any late-evening errands like grocery shopping done, shower, and then pack an overnight bag. When I actually had time to do things like grocery shop, it was always rushed and like watching a contestant on *Supermarket Sweep* having a seizure over the produce aisles. By the time I finished and found street parking at Mark's place, which was often near 10:00 p.m., I was ready for bed, but fully aware that if I were going to spend time with him, I would need to stay awake for a couple hours more.

After a few months (as it so often goes with the post-honeymoon stage), Mark began to complain about the footboard of my bed. He was tall and his feet extended over it, which he said bothered his ankles and caused him to have a hard time sleeping. I threw blankets and pillows over the edge, so that he could rest his ankles more comfortably, but he insisted it was easier for me to spend the night at his house and that we could both sleep better in his bed. The new arrangement was, of course, easier for Mark all around—he never had to wake up earlier for work, miss watching a game with his roommates, or worry about packing lunches the night before.

I eventually ended up giving in, because I loved Mark and because I wanted to spend all of my time with him, no matter whose house we stayed at. Sure, the footboard of my bed cut into his ankles, but our new arrangement cut into my time, and I never pushed back. At that very specific moment, I had begun to de-prioritize myself and my own needs, and I only had myself to blame.

By the second year into our relationship, the good still far outweighed the bad, and I continued to love, hard. We moved in together and our relationship became true bliss: bye-bye overnight bags! Now, I could walk five feet to my own dresser and open a drawer to pull out clothes. I could rummage through shelves of cosmetics instead of travel bags to get ready, and I even housed all my food under one roof—in the fridge!

Man, I really had it made.

Mark and I even routinely cooked dinners together and sat outside on the deck and, on one night, I lit more than fifty tea candles and sprinkled them out by our feet, so it was like we were looking down at a sky full of twinkling stars. I finally had what I always prayed for and planned for, a home and my prince charming. Everything was finally going my way. Everything felt perfect.

Speaking of homes, Mark and I lived together in a small neighborhood in Baltimore City, known for its crime—but also its quaint, historical row homes, paired with a horrific lack of parking. The joke is that there's either a bar or a church on every corner, and I'll just say that my faith was lacking in the attendance category. When Mark and I should have been sharing values, we were sharing mimosas over brunch. We lived in-the-now, and we were the fun couple that everyone wanted to be.

Eventually, I began to see my finances take a hit, and I begrudgingly reeled back. I had blown through more than $10,000 in savings and needed to grow up, quick. I took on more freelancing jobs in addition to my day job, and landed some solid gigs. I went out less and worked more.

I won't go much further into Mark, because this is my story—not his. But to explain what led to our breakup, I will say that we really started to fight when approaching our third year together. Before, we never fought, because there wasn't anything to ever fight about when you're having fun. Now, our fights ran on a continuous loop, and I became very critical of Mark. I felt as if the relationship wasn't evolving as we grew older.

"Is an engagement going to be in our future?" I kept asking. I wasn't in my early twenties anymore. I was 30 years old, soon to be 31 by that time, and I wanted to understand where my future was headed.

"What's the rush?" Mark asked. He always responded by accusing me that I needed a timeline to get engaged. "We're together, and you know we're going to get married. Why does everything always have to be planned, and why can't we be happy and enjoy the moment?"

When you're older, and no matter what anyone tells you, asking about an engagement and the future of your relationship is a topic that should be discussed. Those are fair questions to ask when you're in a serious relationship. You've had time to grow into yourself—unlike during your early twenties, when you're still figuring out which job you even want. Now of course, you don't want to press a relationship if it's not ready, and you want to give it ample time to grow. But, at some point, you have to acknowledge that you have more responsibilities as an older adult. The time that I gave to Mark was substantial—and so I naturally had less time to spend with my family and friends, and less time to develop myself as a writer. That's what happens when you're in a relationship, because it's ultimately worth it. And so, it was only fitting that I wanted to affirm that my investment could mature. Shouldn't we be excited? I wanted to learn how we could grow even stronger as a team.

I stood my ground whenever we fought, and always responded to Mark that his timeline didn't include a commitment to me, despite the fact that we were already living together. I certainly understood that relationships move at their own pace, and I knew couples who wanted to work out their differences before getting hitched, which sometimes took years and years. I admired their determination and commitment to each other. But just like with Mark's argument that every couple is different, I knew that I would never be the individual who could wait to become engaged after five, ten, or fifteen years.

I knew, deep down, that Mark and I had diverged to two very different points in our lives and, marriage talk aside, we each carried very different priorities. Our arguments never stopped cycling, and only temporarily paused from time to time.

Mark was right in some ways when he blamed me for not cutting him enough slack. Especially with regard to relationships, recognizing and relishing in the good parts of life are always pressed upon us because positivity can be a freeing mindset. Human nature by default is overly critical and, when we focus on the positive, we're able to appreciate that much more of a person. In going off of this mentality, you might remember the age-old saying, "It's the little things that count." But I'm a firm believer that this mantra runs both ways: little thoughts of consideration count in making a person feel special and loved. At the same time, little acts of selfishness add up, and I was whittled down.

One evening, I needed to get away from Mark and from everyone. I checked in at a motel near my work, one that I could afford. The front door had a funny lock to it and the paper thin sheets felt like my big toe could rip open a hole in them at any time, and I understood then why the rates were $49/night. I fell asleep to the TV, but I jumped awake to my own thoughts throughout the night. Could the lock be jimmied? Is someone watching me through a double-sided mirror? I felt like Keith Morrison on *Dateline* was waiting to narrate my every move.

And then, when I eventually couldn't fall back asleep, the detached voice in my head asked:

What are you doing here? What… are you doing?

I was so low. So blue. My lowest point wasn't whenever I fought with Mark—it was that night in the motel, when I was finally alone and able to process my thoughts. I was unhappy. We were both unhappy.

One weekend, not too long after my breaking point and when I was supposed to travel with Mark to a wedding, I cancelled my flight and told him that I had to do what was best for me, and we both knew what that meant. He didn't even try to fight it, because it was a relief for both of us. We were both finally free to find our own peace.

We took rotations in the apartment to pack up our belongings, though neither of us had actually figured out where we were moving yet, and my heart ached to look at the empty space. We were breaking up. I was single. Things were done. It was over. The sentiment was in such stark contrast to when we first moved in together, which I thought signified the start of years and even decades to come. We had developed sentimental routines, like with me, trying to covertly push Mark's shirts to the right to make way for more of mine in our closet, but with him always noticing and moving his clothes back over. Or with his favorite cookies, which he always put on the very top shelf so that I couldn't reach them. None of that mattered anymore.

We may have hugged at the end. I really can't remember, but I do know that neither of us broke down. I didn't cry because the breakup had been a long time coming, and I was numb and relieved for my joint tenancy to finally come to an end.

As I packed up trash bags and boxes of my belongings, I thought that our breakup would be the peak of my turmoil. I thought that all of the hatred that I felt, the hatred that embodied me and infiltrated every word that I had spoken would lift. That it would all float away from me and I would feel an automatic rush of peace.

I wanted that ZzzQuil warm-and-happy kind of feeling. I expected it.

But... I never got it right away, at least not like I had hoped. I didn't understand then, at the time, that I needed to look at myself first. And, if you're like me and currently feeling the worst of the worst, and experiencing emotions you never thought you had, remember this: there's nothing wrong with processing life.

You *will* get over your breakup. It *will* happen.

But, just know that it won't magically happen one morning, or one day next week, no matter how many two-second self-help lists you read in between

TV commercials. Not every part of life is happy and full of butterflies—and not every happy moment in life unfolds immediately… and this, yes, is coming from a happiness writer.

Now, I finally understand that life will never, and can never, be a constant explosion of happy social media posts. Sometimes, life requires that we take the bad with the good. Life's happenings—well, they happen. And when you are able to finally get to the point where you can acknowledge that not all days need to be bubble-gum-glib, like I once thought—that's the first and most important step to launching the healing process, and to really understanding that that's a more genuine kind of life.

3

Moving on Up
(and Out—Twice)

What's the most difficult thing about a breakup?

Besides the roller coaster ride of missing and then hating your ex-boyfriend (or ex-girlfriend), it's the immediate need to uproot your life.

If you're like most couples in your thirties, you're living together and so this makes a breakup even more complicated. It's not as technically involved as a divorce, no, because I didn't need to sell a house and divide up my assets. But what my friends didn't realize was that there were still legal technicalities that were an absolute brain aneurysm of a nightmare. For me, that mainly included getting out of a joint tenancy and having to pay $10,000 dollars in penalty fees in a relatively short period of time.

That's right, folks: *ten thousand* dollars.

Why so much in penalties, when you're just a renter—you might ask?

Here's the answer: leases are tricky bitches. Read all of the fine print before you sign. Since we were now breaching our lease, and moving out earlier than the period we initially committed to on paper, we were required to pay back our concessions or free incentives dating back to when we first signed the lease. That meant that we owed months and months of free parking in the covered garage (a super costly expense, given living in the city), and that we were also legally mandated to pay out two months' worth of rent as penalty fees, plus two months' worth of rent as "advanced notification of our termination."

I spoke to a handful of real estate agents, and they recommended that I ride out the rest of my lease in shifts to avoid having to take that big of a dent to my bank account. Others recommended subletting, but then warned that we'd have to draw up an independent contract, and bank on strangers:

    a) Not trashing the apartment during the rest of the lease, so that we'd get our security deposit back,

    b) Having good credit and being trustworthy enough (either way, we'd still have to pay an attorney to draw up an independent subletting lease), and

    c) Making the rent payments directly to us, because we'd have to continue to pay the apartment complex as the original signees to the lease.

If we wanted to go this route, that would mean putting out ads, interviewing subletters, setting up meetings with an attorney, and then touching bases each month to acquire rent payments from the subletters in advance, so that we'd have money in our accounts to then pay the rent.

I was already exhausted, and the process would knowingly add more to my already maxed out mental load. Would this be worth it? Should I go through with it?

Financially, I knew that the answer was yes. But mentally, I knew that I couldn't endure living with Mark any longer and that I didn't want to be tied down to him in any way, and certainly not for another six months or so. Even if we decided to take shifts, I didn't want to sleep in a bed that smelled like him, or look at all of his T-shirts that I used to wear as pajamas. Though it pained me to admit that I wasn't strong enough to make it through the rest of the year, I needed to realistically take the financial cut and walk away.

One evening, as I was packing up my stuff, I felt the urge to walk to the front office and candidly speak to our property manager, woman to woman. I explained that I was going through a break up. I was embarrassed, but I wanted to see if there were any options besides subletting. She confirmed that there weren't, because she didn't have the power to override our contract, no matter how bad she felt for our situation.

I remember staring at her and thanking her, and then we both pursed our lips at each other, as if to say, "Well, shit." I felt out of body. I went back upstairs and began drafting the mandated joint letter of termination, and started budgeting to pull out money from my bank accounts.

A few days later, our property manager called me. She found a loophole in the process that could let us off of the hook, enabling us to both move out and forego having to pay our penalty fees—all $10,000 worth: she could release our apartment to a couple wanting to replace their view of the dumpsters with our view of the courtyard. The stipulation? We just had one, maybe two weeks—tops—to find new places to each live, finish splitting up our stuff, and move the hell out. Had I approached our manager one week earlier or two weeks later, we may not have had that option, and I would have been $10,000 in the hole.

Timing is everything.

I quickly searched for apartments that would allow an immediate move-in, nixing the his-and-her sinks and going for the one-bedroom that would house... well, just me. After touring every viable complex, I was finally delighted to find a unit within my price range, fitted with a washer and dryer, and located only a half-hour away from work. I needed to move out of the city. I needed to shake off years of memories.

The thought of needing to scramble to pack and then move—and by myself this time, was a daunting task. It's also an extremely heavy task if you're a writer like me, because consolidating multiple 600-page manuscript drafts and binders of clips into boxes is a hefty load to tow.

If you're also like me and need to move… hopefully, you have more than two weeks. I have moved five times in the past five years, and am a seasoned pro on moving, and moving efficiently.

Still feeling overwhelmed? Well, here are my moving tips:

1) Grocery store circulars are great for wrapping dishes.[2*] Even better—instead of wrapping individual plates in paper, stick Styrofoam plates in between each plate for cushioned, easy moving.

2) If you have a shortage of moving boxes, ask a local liquor store if they can spare any extra heavy-duty boxes. They'll typically throw them away, anyways. (Just keep in mind that there may not be top-closing panels.) You can also check with a nearby office or building manager for boxes. Empty copy paper boxes are sturdy and have lids, which are perfect.

3) If you have the money, purchase large, cheap plastic bins like the kind Rubbermaid makes for storage purposes. Pack them according to how you want the items stored and, once you're in your new place, you won't have to worry about re-sorting through your stuff—just simply store the bins away. I even bought

---

[2*] Instead of spending money to buy newsprint to wrap my fragile items, I may have quickly run into the front entrances of multiple grocery stores one evening to take all of their weekly circulars.

clear sheet protectors and made signs for each bin, and stuck them on with glue dots. Best of all? The bins are stackable and can be packed heavy, so long as you have a handcart to roll them away.

4) When it comes to your closet, think drawstring trash bags: chunk your closet into sections of clothing about a foot wide. Take a clean trash bag, turn it upside down, so the bottom of the bag is at the top—and cut a small hole in the center of the bottom of the bag, just large enough so that you can run the hooks of your hangers through. Then, tie up the drawstring of your trash bag, which should now be level with the bottom hems of your clothes, to prevent any shirts or dresses from completely slipping out.

Once you're in your new place, hang up the bags, carefully cut or rip open down the length of the bag—and then, ta-dah! Your clothes are now hanging in order, exactly as you had them, and you've saved yourself from the unfolding and folding and tangled hanger debauchery.

5) Buying lunch, dinner, or drinks for the friends who help you move can add up. Instead of taking each person out individually, pop out early to pick up bagels and to-go cartons of coffee. Later, bribe those same helpers to stick around for lunch by ordering pizza and beer. And, don't forget to bring cups for water.

6) Packing up each room in a clockwise direction kept me the most focused, and that's typically how I asked friends to help me as well. I also kept one or two

boxes out, front and center, which were the designated "VALUABLE" boxes. That way, I didn't need to handle every box or bag with care, and I knew which ones contained my glass-blown flowers from Bermuda or other sort of breakable sentiment.

The Post-Move Aftermath

I had assumed all along that my next move would be with Mark and into our first house, so the move to an apartment, alone, was deflating. I had never lived alone. And, according to everyone that I knew who had gone through either a divorce or breakup, the transition to living alone was the most frightening concept— more than the breakup itself.

Now, as the urgency to move had dissipated, and my friends who had helped me move naturally moved on to their own lives, I was left to settle into my apartment with just my thoughts. I'm naturally averse to silence in general, and so moving into a new place without the immediate setup of TV or the Internet was extremely unsettling and lonely.

I had only brought one DVD with me for some reason: Katy Perry's *Part of Me*. I listened to it on loop on my laptop, over and over and over again, as I color-coded my socks to the tune of "Teenage Dream" and reinflated my air mattress to "I Kissed a Girl." I no longer had a regular mattress, or a bedframe, or a TV, couch, or kitchen table. And so I tried my best to enjoy spreading out my clothes in my new walk-in closet, this time on both sides. I also tried to remind myself that I should be proud of my newfound independence. But, at the end of the day, I also had to be completely honest with myself: my new apartment sucked. I was barely scraping by to afford a beat-down shoebox, and it was a drastic down-grade from my old one that had been equally afforded by two salaries and in the heart of the city.

I know that I sound spoiled. I missed the gym, coffee bar, resident nights, the chaise lounges and the courtyard, and the location and convenience of... everything. I missed my friends. I missed being com-fortable. And as much as it pained me to admit, I missed my old life.

My friend, Jeanette, is the perfect example of all of this. She's exceptionally strong willed—to the point of carrying both a USB drive and a full-fledged utility knife (it's more of a kit) in her very expensive purses, wherever she goes. She finally broke down, during her divorce, when she moved out of her cushy four-bed-room home and into a one-bedroom apartment in the basement of a complex. She had to immediately down-size, and threw away a lot of her plants in her green-house... ones that she had raised for years and years.

"That fern's been my longest relationship," she said. I thought it was a tad bit dramatic that the photo that she sent me was of the fern in the actual garbage, but I got it. Bitterness can do that to you.

Space and storage issues are generally the next obstacle during these types of transitions: Jeanette had to rent out a storage unit to hold her grandfather's antique furniture, and her apartment was not large enough to house her china cabinet and collection of Cartier salt and pepper shakers. She cried when she had to get used to her new noisy neighbors as well as a faucet that bubbled up with brown water whenever she flushed the toilet. One evening, when she was sitting on that very toilet and was (for some reason) texting me, she found "I hate my life" etched in the edge of her bathroom counter by some former tenant.

During my own move, I had contemplated taking our old couch with me, but I didn't want to remember where Mark always sat, or look at it and then think about how we spent our weekends binging on *Entourage* or *OITNB*. I experienced some initial hesitation over my need to exercise a controlled level of fiscal responsibility, but then I thought about what I wanted and eventually ordered a brand new gray sectional with a subtle chevron detail. I then figured that a brand new couch required a decent TV, so I ordered a 55 inch. Mark had the same size or a little smaller, and I didn't want to cut myself short by even an inch… so, I didn't.

Both major purchases were to be delivered within the first few days after my move. All I can say is, thank goodness for interest-free payment plans and Amazon credit cards.

The kitchen was the hardest part to unpack. I am not a serious cook, and so the logistics of where spices and plates should be stored were beyond me. I stacked heavy pots and pans on the high shelves, over my head, and mentally noted to purchase dinnerware because Mark had taken it with him… yet another expense. And as I wiped down the kitchen cabinets and lovingly nestled my silverware into drawers, I noticed what should have been my first screaming alarm bell: a white powder, the consistency of confectioner's sugar, smeared on the sides of the drawers as I pulled them out. When I rubbed my fingers together, the powder had a strangely dry feeling to it, like a chalky sawdust. But I shrugged, figuring it was remodeling residue, and I continued to wipe down everything with sanitizing wipes.

By the first week, my sectional was delivered and assembled, and so was my TV. I hung my mirrors and frames. I bought new throw pillows, lamps, end tables, and curtains and rods, and I got my cable and Internet hooked up and running. I did what I could, and my apartment surprisingly looked like it was straight out of Pinterest in no time. I couldn't help but to feel proud of myself. I had picked up and moved on without even blinking.

My routine was still new and living alone on the ground floor was frightening, so my father graciously installed window alarms and locks, and even then pieces of wood to wedge in each horizontal sliding track. It was still an adjustment, but I was beginning to feel more and more comfortable.

Just not 100%.

In addition to the white powder in the kitchen, I noticed something very strange that first week: every morning on my white bathroom counters, bits of peppery-looking residue appeared. Before I left for work, I wiped down the counters and, when I returned home, my counters remained clean. However, as if elves were magically working overnight, the same sprinkles reappeared every morning.

On top of that, when I was cooking dinner that first weekend, I opened the fridge to find two inch-long brownish streaks near my pans of uncovered food that I had been eating out of during the week. I shrugged, thinking nothing of it, and assumed that the bottom of the pan was just dirty. I wiped the shelf off, and then poured myself a glass of wine to enjoy while sitting on my brand new couch and watching some trashy reality show on my brand new TV. Nothing, I tell you, beats a fresh purchase—one that you can claim, "Mine. Mine. Mine," after a breakup.

The next day, I woke up around noon, living the good life and still sprawled out on my couch with the TV on, and I caught sight of a beetle quickly scurrying up the wall where my TV was plugged in. This particular scenario alarmed me for two reasons:

I am deathly afraid of all bugs, and I never thought beetles moved so fast. I thought they were slow bugs that always died when they got flipped over on their backs.

Half groggy and cringing, I crept up behind the bug with a wadded paper towel, and that's when I noticed that the beetle had very long antennae.

What was this? A water bug?

But before I could lower the paper towel even remotely near it, it zip-zipped away into my heating vent. Immediately, the second alarm bell sounded. I had never seen an insect, let alone a beetle or similarly looking water bug, move so fast and know how to escape so quickly. Also, I wasn't near water and that ruled out the latter nomenclature.

Out came the iPhone and up came Google: *What is a fast moving beetle?* I frantically typed.

My phone instantly flooded with images… images of roaches. Roaches!

Roaches!

…Roaches…

Me, always naïve, thought, *but what if it's just one?*

I kept reading. "If you see a roach during the day, that's a sign of a severe infestation." And then, "If you notice what looks like coffee grounds or black pepper…"

Oh.

I began to cry so hard that I eventually gave myself hives for two days, mostly because I had no idea what to do. I dealt with mainly ants, mice, and even rats when I lived in the city, and I could deal just fine with all of them. But roaches? It was a true phobia. Part of me wondered if I should tough it out, because it was apartment living, after all, and any sort of bug was just part of reality. I had manically apartment hunted, and most other units were not in my price range. Plus, the thought of moving—packing and unpacking, *again!*—was overwhelming. I had just taken off of work to move and hadn't accrued more time off yet.

The other half of me second guessed my newfound independence: did I make the right decision? Should I move in with friends? Or worse yet, gulp—*home*?

Well, when I tell you that week that I tossed and turned over my decision, I literally did, mainly because I was still sleeping on an air mattress on the ground. I bought several cans of Raid and sprayed the carpeting surrounding my bed in a thick line, and I prayed that an apartment complex fire or some flickering spark wouldn't ignite—because I'd combust. Always the extremist, I kept envisioning myself as some sacrificial token on a plastic air mattress altar, igniting into a slab of flames from the highly flammable Raid that I kept spraying around my bedding.

My couch was now a new matter. When I sat on it, I was aware of every spot on my walls, carpeting, and sofa cushions, and the moving spots—well, they were the worst. I sat with wadded up paper towels and noticed something else, something new: trails of baby bugs, everywhere. Whenever I entered the kitchen, I cringed even more because now I understood that the white powder wasn't confectioner's sugar from the former tenant, whom I had imagined was a plump and avid baker. The residue was from a roach bomb.

In standard Lisa fashion, I of course hadn't cried over my breakup, even though I dreaded coming home to Mark. Now that I dreaded coming home to my apartment, which was supposed to finally be my personal safe haven, I publicly sobbed. I sobbed getting ready in the morning and silently cried behind my desk at work. Whenever my new colleagues asked me what was wrong, I lied and told them that I had allergies, though the amount of tears streaming down my face clearly indicated otherwise. Once I got home, I flinched whenever I had to shake roaches out of my blankets and cried some more. I was running off of fumes and anxiety, and that was about it.

One evening when I was about to wash the dishes, I closed my eyes in prayer. "Please—God, just give me a sign to tell me what to do." And when I picked up my dish sponge, away ran four unwanted friends, and I had my answer.

The next weekend, the complex let me cancel my lease, no questions asked, and I began apartment hunting… again. I felt duped that things hadn't worked out the first time.

I cancelled my utilities and cable, and absorbed the early cancellation charges. Oh and I began packing, again… except this time, I didn't ask any of my friends for help. I refused to, because I was too embarrassed. I wanted everyone to think that I was naturally thriving—and not living in some roach motel-level dump. This time around, I channeled all of my fury (and I mean all of it) into packing. I shook out all of my clothes and checked inside all of my dishes, which took twice as long. I packed as much as I could into huge, sealed Ziploc bags and even more into Rubbermaid bins, and I dropped roach traps in everything… just in case, because I didn't want to bring any bugs with me. Oh, and, I cried the whole time while I was doing it.

Despite the inconveniences of the first move, time was on my side for the second: I stumbled upon a brand new apartment complex with available units, a building so new that I had completely missed it the first time. The building had security cameras and badge-swipe entrances, and was also several hundred more a month for half of the living space, which happened to be five hundred square feet and positioned in an awkward L-shape. But all's well that ends well—right? I was able to move in the day that I signed my lease, and I did just that.

In conclusion, the following is an addendum to my helpful hints on moving for a second time.

1. Listen to everything that the friendly people at Ace Hardware have to say, especially about bugs.
2. Ask your neighbors if they like living where they are… before you move in.
3. And finally, don't tell your friends about anything, because they will not want you over their homes or want to visit your new place. Ever.

4

The Bad and the Ugly

I took a week to unpack and a month to finally feel settled into my new apartment, take two. I finally felt safe. My place was clean. Yes, I had to place my 55-inch TV less than three feet away from my couch, but I chose to view watching my TV as... you know, a heightened cinematic IMAX experience. I also felt slightly claustrophobic that my bed was less than six feet away from the stove but, on the positive side, at least I could ditch the cans of Raid without worry.

My life had momentarily stabilized. I was no longer on an adrenaline high, doggy paddling to stay above water. I had broken up with Mark. I even moved twice. I thought the end of all of my sadness was near, and I was eagerly ready for whatever was next.

Unfortunately, as a writer, my thoughts never stop. I wake up in the morning, read headlines, and write all day. I'm forced to consider all perspectives and question each one. I stress over what clause should come next and worry if I'll have enough content for the future. I reread what I've written, overanalyze it, edit it, and then rewrite it. I'm good at it. I'm a successful writer *because* my mind never shuts off. It's my job to be both hyper-proactive and hyperanxious, as well as overly critical of myself, but those facets of my personality are hard to turn off when I'm not working.

Post-breakup, I was still in surprised shock that I hadn't reached my state of calm yet. I make a living writing about mental mindsets, and in an abbreviated fashion for the online forum. I practiced my controlled, meditated breathing in just ten steps and in just five minutes—but I was still jittery, upset, and anxious. Where was my happiness? As a perfectionist, I not only wanted to feel happy all of the time, but I also expected it. I was entitled to it, wasn't I?

Suddenly though, the opposite happened: my body became increasingly uncontrollable by two-fold, both in the mental and physical senses. When an emotional stressor like a breakup happens, my neuroses flare in full force. Not only had I lost control of my dwelling, looping thoughts, but I started to experience what I call the Burning Feelings.

Here's what I mean.

I look at emotions like joy and happiness as effervescent feelings that make us feel bubbly and make us laugh. They're the pleasant spectrum of emotions that we all want to experience. But on the other end are what I call the Burning Feelings, which are the worst of them all and what you'll, no doubt, experience—if you aren't already. The Burning Feelings make your shins and toes tingle with anxiety and fill your cheeks with red, smoldering anger. Fear makes you drench yourself with hot sweat in the middle of the night, so that your cotton T-shirt sticks to you like plastic wrap. Worry makes the pit of your esophagus and your stomach churn, no matter how many antacids you take. Those are the Burning Feelings. Those are the physical emotions that you'll experience during your lowest of lows.

Of them all? Fear was the worst. It crept up on me during life's little pauses and interrupted my sleep at night. My greatest fear is to be alone, and my thoughts never stopped reminding me of that.

I also needed to adjust to my disrupted routine. I'm a planner and thrive on productive consistency, and so it didn't help that I had based my entire being and schedule around Mark. He kissed me good night and good morning, and he had been my support system for more than three years. We lived and had made a home together, and I missed the comfort of always having someone else in the apartment… and basically in every single moment, big and small, of my life.

I missed the future of Mark even more, and I couldn't stop comparing my loneliness to the times we spent together. I felt like I was starring in some really sad slow-motion movie.

"You're lucky you still have a semblance of who you even are," another friend, who was going through a divorce, said to me one day. "I've melded so much into Jon that I don't know who I am. I stopped making big, independent decisions a long time ago. Everything hurts, like when I go to paint nights by myself, and I don't even know what initials to paint in the bottom corner."

She called me when she took her ring back to the jeweler to have it disassembled, so that she could give the diamond back to her ex-husband.

"What will they do with the setting?" I asked.

"They'll melt it down to make new jewelry for happier people and happier couples," she said, laughing, but I looked to the ground when she said it.

When they had to get lawyers involved about titles and transfers, she opened up to me about her debt and bankruptcy filings.

"That's the thing about a divorce," she added. "It's stuff. Emotional stuff. Dividing up stuff. Moving stuff. Rearranging stuff."

Now, to stare at my new closet, with my stuff spread out on both sides, was one of the most foreign of feelings. Even though my apartment was small and I had Rubbermaid bins stacked up to the ceiling, it still felt empty because I now had half of the stuff that I had when Mark and I were living together. I bitterly looked back on when I unpacked our first apartment, way back when, and lined up our shoes together. To now see only my heels in one line in my empty closet triggered an exponential amount of sadness.

This isn't how it was supposed to turn out, I thought. Where was our happy ending? Where is my happy ending? I mean, didn't I write about this kind of stuff?

The late nights and early mornings were the worst for me—right before I started to fall asleep or was just coming to, still drowsy. It's when we're at our most vulnerable and when I really needed someone, because I feel like that's the time when couples share their secrets, their affection, or at least say what they really want to say. It's when our guards are down, when we whisper to each other, and when everything stops for a second.

I missed falling asleep against Mark at night, in the nook of his outstretched arm and up against his neck. I knew he'd never lean down again to kiss me goodbye, right before he left for work. I'd always pretend to be sleeping, only to playfully spring up at him, wrapping my arms and legs around him to prevent him from leaving. And I missed how, whenever he would wake, he would stretch his arms out to pull me in closer, up against his chest.

One night, a month or so after our breakup and when I was feeling particularly blue, I smelled my pillow that Mark always slept on and the woosh of his sweat and cologne flooded my senses. It was almost like an out-of-body experience, like I had just closed my eyes to watch a movie montage. *Just go to sleep*, I kept telling myself, over and over again, as if I were counting sheep. But then I thought about his hairline and his big ears, and the mole on his arm. He was a ghost. I wanted to let him go, but I couldn't. I just didn't understand how someone that I hated so much could leave such a void. I couldn't make sense of it.

What I hated myself for even more was that I still fantasized about rewinding time or thought about what it would feel like to have him back. It didn't matter that I knew that I didn't love him anymore. That we had broken up. His presence had a funny way of unexpectedly slipping into my thoughts, like whenever I went grocery shopping and strolled past the specific boxes of crunchy protein bars that Mark always ate. Right in the middle of the aisle, I would suddenly find myself laughing, remembering about how he would hide those and his favorite cookies by the fridge, assuming I would never find them. But I always pulled myself back to reality when I realized that Mark wouldn't be there for me anymore and that we would never make new memories. I had to remind myself of that during instances like when I unpacked my toothbrush and then thought about the pink toothbrush holder that we shared. Afterwards, I cursed myself for allowing something so trivial to trigger my thoughts.

Triggers eventually became so immediate that, even if I saw a frying pan, I would begin to vividly replay, say, the time I made a frittata in the pan for the both of us one evening. *Towel.* His towel that I accidentally bleached with my face wash. *Skirt.* The one that ripped when he lifted me up over his head one Sunday morning. *Rug.* The one he spilled beer on. *Muffin tin.* The time I went through a phase and made rounds and rounds of mini-meatloaves and mini-pot pies. Mini-everythings.

I missed Mark and his companionship, but I couldn't pick and choose which parts of a person I could keep. The good comes with the bad, and the bad comes with the ugliest parts of a person. But for some reason, I only kept fantasizing about the best moments. Why do we do that to ourselves?

Probably because it's easier to miss the moments that made you feel like the luckiest person alive.

I couldn't help but to reminisce over my most recent birthday with Mark. I kept replaying it over and over: I came home from work that day, and Mark had pretended to forget my birthday. An hour after my face had fully dropped, he pulled out a gift bag from behind the couch. Instead of using tissue paper, he had stuffed the bag with squares of toilet paper, a funny joke that I got, since he constantly griped at how much toilet paper I always wasted. I remember digging through the bag, like a hamster unburying a treat, until I pulled out a slippery purple Ravens jersey. I held it up, admiring the netting and the thick stitching. Mark even put my name on the back, and it was my first football jersey ever. I had always wanted one, but I felt too guilty spending the money.

That evening, I think my smile was almost as big as the Christmas morning when my parents gifted me with a pink vanity filled with school supplies. Who needed makeup as an eight year old? Certainly not a dork like me.

Mark tapped me on the nose and pulled me in against the scruff on his chin, and I remember feeling really, really loved that birthday. The prior year when the Ravens won an important playoff game, we walked through the streets and he had put me on his shoulders so I was safe, away from the drunks and thrashing elbows. I was able to look down on the whole town as a purple screaming sea, and our hometown football team became so much more to me that year.

"Happy birthday, puppy," he said. "I love you."

I can still see that evening. Him, on the brown couch and me, on the splintering hardwood floor, surrounded by shreds of toilet paper. I can *feel* that evening, like how perfect I felt when the jersey fit me to a T. I can feel myself hooking my arms around his neck and lifting myself up on him, so that I could wrap my legs around his waist.

Later that night, we met up with my friends and I felt out of body. I finally had someone who knew me inside and out, and I distinctly recall how incredible it felt to realize that I would never have to spend another birthday alone. That I would always have someone to come home to and who would make even every day an intimate one. I was so invincible then.

But that was then.

Now, all I had left were fantasies intermingled with fits of anger as I sat in my apartment in silence.

Alarm clock. The one I threw when he didn't come home one evening.

Blanket. The fringed one he used when he slept on the couch.

Remote. The main controller I was never allowed to touch.

In addition to my triggers, walking into a dark home and having to flip on all of the lights to feel safe was embarrassing. Instead of slinging my bags on our hand-me-down armchair and then divulging the details of my day, I came home to silence, flipped on the TV for background noise, and then thought:

What have I done? Will this be worth it?

I almost needed Mark to say, "You should break up with me. That was the right thing to do… you know we weren't happy." That just wasn't reality, though.

The breakup and moves had happened so quickly, within a matter of weeks, and so the abrupt silence of my apartment was lonely and frightening. I didn't know how to be alone. I had been used to a soundboard and talking to Mark on a non-stop basis. I was still acting on reflex, and could feel myself wanting to pick up the phone to text him whenever something good or bad happened—it was really strange and painful, like how I imagine someone feels when they experience the death of a loved one. The silence, the cooking shows that I spaced out to… it all highlighted the new void in my life. And, I finally understood how underrated face-to-face conversations are these days, like with the question, "How was your day?" Because it's so standard, it's often ignored. Well, I can't count how many times I simply responded with a shrug and a "good" to the question once I walked through the door. Sometimes, I even ignored it altogether and gave a scowl to sum up my day. I didn't have anyone to talk to anymore... not even to look at. I missed my soundboard. I missed the routine conversations with my legs swung over his on the couch. I missed Mark's body heat and the comfort of his chest rising and falling with each breath. I missed the heat of his kiss.

My social life had also gone to shit. On top of everything else, I realized that I had nothing to do— no recurring plans. I had no one to go out to dinner with or watch movies with whenever I wanted, on the fly, and so I felt like Friday nights through Sundays were outstretched amounts of time. Once Saturday hit, I slept in until I was hungry and headachy, and until the back of my head throbbed because I had chosen to sleep for close to fourteen hours. When I finally did manage to wake up, which was routinely past two in the afternoon, I was often drenched with sweat from having wrapped myself in the thick of my comforter and from the anxious, sweaty bouts I experienced upon waking and rewaking. Sleeping was my comfort. I could temporarily shut off my thoughts.

Of course I never admitted to my friends that I was having a hard time. Most had encouraged me to stay with them in the city and in the middle of the hub-bub of it all to stay connected to people my age. Had I stayed, I could have easily shacked up with friends for near to nothing, or found a random roommate to cut my rent in half or even in thirds. But the truth was, I also needed to take a break from my former social life. I didn't want to surround myself with friends and force myself to become so busy that my eyes blurred. I needed to be alone, and so I budgeted to stay within my means and even picked up a steady part-time freelancing job to help pay the rent.

Many of my best friends told me how much they admired me for moving on and for not settling. But I took what they had to say with a grain of salt, because I feared being single at a time when most of my friends were transitioning to such different stages in their lives. Almost all of my friends were either married (or had been married), were engaged, or in long-term relationships. Many of them already had children and some were planning for their second child. I knew that comparison was unhealthy, and so was the rat race of keeping up with the Joneses. But can I also be honest with you? I was embarrassed of where I felt like I was in life, and I felt like I had nothing to show for it.

I thought that walking away from a detrimental relationship proved maturity, but it still seemed to raise a lot of questions from friends, including those I hadn't talked to in a while, and I felt judged. Out of the blue, and I guess she picked up on my silence on Facebook, I had a former coworker text me three different times, asking, "What happened?" It was over the course of a few weeks, and there was nothing more to the texts. Prior to that, we hadn't talked in years.

The funny thing is, when relationships fail, people always want to know why—it's the first question they ask. Sometimes, you'll get a follow-up, "How are you doing?" Other times, you won't. Anyways, I didn't answer, because I didn't owe her an answer.

I also started becoming angry. I was angry at Mark for not being the man I wanted him to be. At myself for not leaving earlier. At my friends for not helping me move, while also wanting to ask so many questions. I was angry that I was alone. One morning, I even became irate that an adolescent barista was short with me. *Doesn't she get that I have very legitimate problems in my life?*

My emotions were becoming more and more uncontrollable. I had stopped showering, so I started dry-shaving my armpits and that wasn't all too comfortable. I had no desire to wear anything but my flannel pajama bottoms and oversized jersey shirts (those were admittedly very comfortable). I had become a cross-combination of a hipster and a hobo.

What was going on with me? I was feeling worse than I did when I was with Mark. I felt like I had taken twelve steps back.

One afternoon, I sat up in my bed and I ran my fingers over my sweat-drenched sheets, which I could have literally wrung out like a washcloth. My mind was against me and antagonizing me, and my body wouldn't stop burning. I was scared. I was terrified to have to depend on myself. I had no one but me. If my day were bad, I had to deal with it. If I were too tired, say, to go to the grocery store, then I had to deal with an empty fridge. I had to own my decisions, whether I wanted to face it or not.

The pessimistic commentator in me continued: *why is everyone... happy?* And what is this sick irony, as a writer, that I'm always dishing advice to others about finding happiness—as it passes me by?

I paused. I realize, now, that I had gradually become very depressed. I just didn't know it then. The simple rituals that so many people take for granted, such as flossing, were extremely physically heavy tasks for me, as if I had a ten-pound weight strapped to my arm.

I walked to the bathroom, stripping off my clothes one by one along the way, and I took an hour-long, scalding hot shower and sat, naked and crumpled up, on the floor. I inhaled the steam and concentrated only on the dripping heat of the water, which finally paused my incessant, neurotic thoughts.

In that small moment, I felt human again. And just that one hour of my life became very important to me: I finally felt in control of my burning anxiety. I knew that I needed to climb out of the mindset that I was entitled to everything... even to my own happiness.

That night, before bed, I gave myself ten minutes to floss my teeth. And after that, with no timeframe in mind, I stripped the sheets off of my bed to change them—a task that, in reality, a healthy person could complete without much thought or effort. Me? Well, I felt like I had taken a muscle relaxer. But I addressed the two outlets that tormented me the most, my mind and body, and I focused on the task at hand—and only that. It suddenly became more manageable to break down each step of changing my bedding, stripping off the left corner with my hand, and then the right, with my knee propped up in the middle of my bed. I thought about the scent of my laundry detergent, and focused on the one time my friend, Stephanie, broke out in full body hives from an allergic reaction to some random, clearance-brand detergent. And then, still laughing, I thought about the YouTube videos I had watched on how to fold a fitted sheet. Maybe one day I would house a closet full of perfectly folded fitted sheets. Maybe. And before I knew it, I got done what I needed to get done, because I forced myself—my mind and my body—to address the situation.

That wasn't really my ah-ha! moment. Maybe it was the match box of the match that lit the candle that ignited the flame. There were much worse things happening out there in the world than my emotions and my breakup, and I knew that, and I knew that I also needed to start getting over myself. I became aware that I needed to start making my time—*my time,* and I knew that the life that I always described so articulately in prose to strangers on the web was screaming for honesty.

And so, it was time. It was time for me to dig up the self-love that I always encouraged, and to stop being a fraud. It was, finally, time to start listening to myself.

5

Let's Make a List

I thought I'd open by detailing the following scenarios:

1) Watching any segment on *Chopped*
2) Using toilet paper that's the consistency of tissue paper
3) Going to Wegmans before a football game
4) Signing up for any group exercise class

If any of these situations raise your blood pressure, then welcome to the high anxiety, compulsive-thinkers club! In order to maintain membership, it's crucial that almost every situation involving another person gives you anxiety and that you consistently over-care what people think about you.

How can you ensure lifetime membership status? Make sure your thoughts never stop obsessing over what you can't control.

If you're like me—a keynote member of this club, I'm sure you understand by now how easy it is to become lost in the post-breakup *what ifs*. What if he could've changed? What if I had stayed? What if I acted too impulsively?

To halt my vicious cycle of thoughts, I continued focusing on the small things that I wanted to get done and it helped my mind to stay occupied. I also took things a step further: I began carrying around several pieces of notepaper with me for list-making purposes, which I kept folded up in my wallet. I highly recommend doing it. While a phone is great for storing your notes, the act of physically hand-writing a list is far more personal and exponentially more definitive, helping you to work on nixing the *what ifs* and reclaiming your thoughts—with confidence. With that said, I kept two running lists:

1) Mark's cons, and
2) My strengths

To start on the first list, think about every con of your former significant other, and write them down all at once. And, laugh all you want at my thoroughness— but, when making my "con" list, I thought about Mark in terms of categories. I wanted it to be comprehensive… and trust me, it was. After your first pass at your list, I would tuck it away for a little bit. Then, once random cons come to mind after that, add them to the list at that exact moment to capture how low or how angry you felt—so that, later, it doesn't become diluted with time.

Remember, though, that this list isn't meant to incur hate and increase episodes of the Burning Feelings. This, my friend, is a self-instituted reality check, designed as a reminder to solidify that where you are is where you need to be. It doesn't matter if you ended a relationship or if you were broken up with: the list also serves as a reminder that the relationship has ended in general. And even if you don't think that it should have ended and you want that person back, there were factors that contributed to it not working out in the long run— whether or not you're willing to believe it. Work on the list. And remember, you're a healthy human being who loves herself or himself, and you're taking back control of your mind. Commit to writing out your thoughts, and you'll no longer be at work with your mind elsewhere, or spending time with your family but scrolling through your phone, reminiscing about the past. You'll get to a point where you'll stop obsessing, and be on your way to fully owning your time. You'll be more at peace with the present.

On New Year's Eve, I specifically needed this list when I was alone and surrounded by sequined and suited-up happy couples. I didn't need to physically read it, because I had it memorized by then, but I needed to at least mentally re-read down the list of Mark's cons to remind myself not to text him.

That night, on the start of a fresh New Year, I envied all of the other couples and wondered if they knew how lucky they had it, being able to go home to the comfort of their own bed and then wake up the next morning to continue their intimate conversations while still buried in their pillows. I hated myself for having to be the awkward female who hovered over other couples' musings, because I had no one else to talk to and nowhere else to stand, and I cringed out of jealousy whenever a fellow female was pulled in closer by her counterpart.

I didn't want Mark for one night. In fact, I didn't want him at all.

These days, we're used to the insta-age. With a few tap-taps of the phone, you can furnish an entire house, order meals and grocery shop online, and even date, picking among categories of Christians, Asians, and farmers. While the premise of partner matching can be a positively life-changing experience, we've simultaneously become accustomed to the realm of insta-men and insta-women. Here, enlarged profile pictures tower over shared interests and morals. And a quick little blurb (if at all) is all the room that we have in order to give the best representation of ourselves. But be careful with the readiness of this trap, and take it from many of my friends: it's not wise to rebound into that next relationship, be it post-breakup or post-divorce. We're still used to getting what we *think* we want, when we want it. But if life were that easy, then these types of dating platforms alone wouldn't have become this multi-million dollar conglomerate. Immediacy doesn't always work out. This time around, take time for yourself.

If you're still having trouble getting started, sit on your couch or on your bed, put away your phone and turn off the TV, and really just think. Purge your emotions and think of all of the lows, and write them down. I warn you that the process will be upsetting and will probably weigh on your mind for several days, but this is an important, cathartic step to get through.

What made you text your friends in fits of venting rages? Or send twenty-three text messages at a time, like I once did? Throw an alarm clock? Again, I emphasize—write down everything. It will help you fight against the urge to text your ex once you've hit the bottle of wine, and remind you that even the *thought* of sex with the ex should be way, way off limits. No contact is key, and that includes defriending and blocking him or her on all social media platforms, no matter how abrupt you might feel that is.

If you're not sure where to begin, just start by setting aside time and making yourself physically sit down to think about what you want to write, before you even know what you have to say. I do it all of the time. Take a deep breath—and release.

Finally, if you need a little kick starter—I'm happy to help.

"The Cons: The Bad and the Ugly"

Cons: _____

_____

Examples: _____

_____

_____

Cons: _____

_____

Examples: _____

_____

_____

Cons: _____

_____

Examples: _____

_____

_____

Cons: _____

_____

Examples: _____

_____

_____

Cons: _____

_____

Examples: _____

_____

_____

Another time that I needed this list was a month later, on Valentine's Day. Call it what you want, like a commercialized marketing ploy by greeting card conglomerates, but that very fusion is what sets my heart on fire—in a good way. The holiday is over-advertised written sentiments, which happens to be exactly my career background: advertising + writing. I'm a prime over-communicator who knows how to sell a message… to death. What could be better than that?

While I can't really tell you what can be better, I can tell you what can be worse… spending a holiday that you hadn't spent alone in a while—alone. I probably spent about four consecutive Valentine's Days with my college boyfriend, who always planned out something thoughtful. One year, he found this little pop-up orchestra that played "My Funny Valentine." On another, he bought me a huge bear and we went to a steakhouse. But I naturally kept focusing to the Valentine's Day dates that Mark and I shared over the years. On the most recent, when we were together, Mark sent me lilies in a square blue vase to work, and we made reservations at a seafood restaurant. I can vividly recall the minute details of the evening, even down to where I had painted my nails red with a gold heart on the ring finger.

"Maybe the next Valentine's Day, I'll have a ring on my finger," I said, sticking out my bare finger, the one with the heart painted on it.

"I'd like to think so," he said back, squeezing my hand.

But now, back to the present: it's so funny how much had changed in just a year from that day. Now that I was alone on Valentine's Day, I wanted to text Mark because it still felt like the default thing to do, and I wanted to see if he missed me. I wanted him to feel as horrible as I felt, and I knew that he was thinking about me. It was such a loaded holiday after all.

What if we both missed each other, and getting back together would only improve things going forward? Maybe we just needed to start talking again...

I sat on my couch and ran my eyes over the details of the cushions, confirming that the subtle chevron was indeed a good choice. So what if I texted him? The worst that could happen is that he wouldn't answer.

Right?

For the next twenty seconds, I closed my eyes and took a deep breath to catch myself up to the present, and then I pulled out "The Bad and the Ugly" from my wallet. I hadn't gone through two moves for nothing. The good comes with the bad. The bad comes with the worst parts of a person. Mark and I had already been through it all, and my friends had already heard about it all. I couldn't let one weak moment make me appear as if I regretted my decision, and that I wanted to come crawling back to him, despite it all. And the truth was, I couldn't let him know that I was having a rough time.

And so I read every reminder of why I needed to be at peace, and then I put down my phone.

I'm never one who likes to stay on low notes, and so to balance out "The Bad and the Ugly," I wrote a list of my strengths—it's still a work in progress to this day. I referred to this list whenever I wondered and replayed what I did wrong, and the process led me to realize that being an anxious perfectionist was a deeply embedded part of me that would never change. My quirks are my quirks. I will never change who I am. There are people who say that loving your flaws means loving yourself, but I find it to be quite the opposite. Instead, by loving yourself first and foremost, you'll be more likely to accept your flaws all around. Here's the exact list that I wrote of my strengths:

1. Work ethic and love for writing
2. Financial independence, like my apartment, sectional, and TV
3. Determination, and down to earth

Though my list has obviously grown since this time, at first listing my TV and sectional felt materialistic—but they marked a unique sense of freedom for me. I could finally sit on *my* couch and watch whatever TV shows *I wanted* to watch, a luxury I had never had before. And, when I wrote the list, I also realized that life could be so much worse. I hadn't even praised my health because that was something that I always took for granted. Instead, I was fixated on the thrills of watching TV alone.

I encourage you to write one more list, like I did, about what you love about yourself. When you're midway through beating yourself up or in need of a pick-me-up, re-reading this list will tip the scale back to your favor, toward the path of onwards and upwards. At first, my list didn't come easy, but I thought about the responsibilities I had as a colleague, friend, daughter, and sister. I mentally skimmed through an average day to brainstorm what helped me get by, like my ability to handle urgent deadlines. I should also stress that you should write this list without the help of your friends, because the point is to write what *you* like about yourself. Give yourself credit where credit is due, and be honest with yourself... you'll find it to be whole-heartedly liberating.

"The Good and the Pretty"

Strength: _____

_____

Examples: _____

_____

_____

Strength: _____

_____

Examples: _____

_____

_____

Strength: _____

_____

Examples: _____

_____

_____

Strength: _____

_____

Examples: _____

_____

_____

Strength: _____

_____

Examples: _____

_____

_____

If you still have problems writing what your strengths are, this should be a sign that you need to prioritize yourself, starting with how you view and think about yourself as a person. How do you do that? Well, that'll take time and practice. For now, don't worry if you're having problems, and work on carving out time to think about yourself and all that you accomplished that day. Maybe that's during the drive home or when you're brushing your teeth before bed, which is what I do and still do. I also actually try really hard not to think about what I have to do the very next day, because then I start to feel rushed with my life. It feels good when you can sit back and say, "Damn. I did good, folks."

As someone who has written both "The Bad and the Ugly" and "The Good and the Pretty," I promise you that writing lists will restore confidence in your decisions and in yourself. Carry them as an extension of your own thoughts, so that you're reminded of yourself. So that you're reminded of your strengths and why you're worthy of good love, starting with the love for yourself. You'll rely on the lists heavily at first but, before you know it, the looping, anxious montage of thoughts will slow down and be replaced with a more thankful, strong outlook. Don't believe me? Well, you should take it from me, and ask anyone who knows me. I know full well that I'm one of the most neurotic individuals out there. The lists work. I don't let my neuroses control my life anymore—instead, I've just learned how to channel them into more productive outlets.

If you need even more evidence, take my friend Jeanette: I recently encouraged her to write these two types of lists while her divorce was pending. While she certainly didn't need to write a list to deter her from her ex-husband, she needed to see what I was talking about and I showed mine to her.

"Lisa. Holy shit. It's a manifesto," she said, laughing.

"No, it's not," I said. "I mean, it's what the experts call self-manifesting. I'm creating a better self. My new self. I mean, OK, it's basically like my Self Manifesto. Is that better?"

Jeanette smiled, and I was glad that I could finally pull one out of her. It had been a while. "Ok, Miss Doc-tour. I guess you're right. I'm going to try this. My Manifest Destiny, where I reclaim my life back and conquer everyone who ever put me down."

"Well, try to take it seriously," I said, "I understand what it's like to move and how tough it all can be." We had been through several rounds of martinis and it had been a good night. You know, the kind where you get sufficiently drunk but you can still be in bed by ten.

While Jeanette did go forward with writing what she disliked about her ex-husband, I don't think she ever wrote what she loves about herself... it's something she really needs to work on. And so, just last week, I gave her a picture frame with her favorite photo of herself in it, and I wrote on the glass for her with a dry erase marker: "Five Reasons Why I Love Myself."

"This should change weekly, my pet," I said. She stared at me and slow blinked a little, just to be annoying, but she knew that I was being serious.

If you're still like Jeanette, well… that's OK. We all move at different paces, and you'll get there—if you want to get there. On the other hand, if you've been able to make it this far, and you've made your lists and checked them twice, then stop and pat yourself on the back. Acknowledge that taking control of your mind is a powerful accomplishment in the healing process. While we don't need to be positive 200% of the time, positivity still needs to be practiced, and that's going to start with one key factor: learning that the "you" is *you*. Now, own it.

6

Hate Hate Hate
(All of Your Friends)

As you've started to ground yourself, I have some particularly bad news: you will begin to resent—if you haven't already—all of your friends. This sentiment might feel like a roadblock, and as a surprising and even alarming feeling, but I guarantee that you will feel this way sooner or later.

Let me explain why.

At first, you will immensely love your tried and true friends even more than normal as you venture through the rituals of a breakup, because they're the ones who have listened to your wavering, "Should I Stay or Should I Go?" lyrical loopings, and they're the ones who have helped you move and have offered up their couches. These people have been the recipients of explicit and randomly timed text rants, and have stepped up to mollify your emotional crises that have, most likely, occurred in the dead of night. What's not to love about them?

But then… hear me out.

Life happens, and theirs continues to move on, while yours is understandably stagnant, having just been interrupted. Their check-in texts or responses become few and far between, because now that we're older, our friends have more pressing priorities—their husbands or wives, children, mortgage payments, and even worries over aging parents. My friends? Admittedly, yes, most of them are married and with children, and so they had their own lives to attend to, as well.

The Great Divide

For me, this is where The Parting of the Seas occurred with my friends. There were those who were busy, but understood that my problems were still upsetting. Then, there were those who made me feel inferior and embarrassed: here I was, upset about a breakup, when there were more pressing matters, like an unexpected daycare closing. And I certainly get it: a dependent's needs, let alone your own child's, certainly trumps all other calls. But the problem with a breakup, particularly at an older age? It sounds juvenile. It feels juvenile. It doesn't seem as final and as devastating as a divorce, and so it's easier to brush off.

On an emotional sense, though? A breakup can be just as tough as a divorce.

Hopefully, most friends will fall into the former category, like mine, but I will be the first to tell you that both situations hurt immensely when the fear of loneliness sets in, causing you to need even more from your friends. I thought back to my early twenties after my very first breakup, when the healing process was staying the weekends with my girlfriends and having them on call whenever I needed them. Ironically enough, breakups near our thirties truly necessitate those types of all-hands-on-deck interventions—even more so than during our twenties. It's just that, as we get older, we find ourselves having less and less time and others, naturally, have less and less time to give.

Now, because of increased life responsibilities and because your friends are busy, you will, deep down, resent everyone. I did. It's a natural combination of jealousy and fear of what's next. I also hadn't chosen to make my relationship my priority—I had chosen to make it my world, and so I resented the happiness of my friends. Most of them had the world I was always trying to grasp. Sure, I appreciated the time that my friends could give me, but I felt as if their genuinely sympathetic words lacked true, experienced understanding. They never needed to fear being alone. None of them. They hadn't for a while.

After my breakup, I had no doubt that my dear friend from college, Lauryn, would be a shoulder to lean on—and she was. We met during freshman year in the study lounge, where I hid out to avoid my roommate and she hid out to avoid hers, who routinely had sex on the top bunk of their bunk beds. We lived together for the next two years after that and our friendship really grew, with her even inviting me to be a bridesmaid in her wedding many years later. I was, and still am, very close with her.

It just so happened that Lauryn found out that she was expecting around the same time I was moving out of my apartment with Mark. Amid her own celebrations and preparations as a first-time mommy, her thoughtfulness grew for me: she stopped over to my new apartment that first week, bearing wine; listened to my meltdowns; invited me over for latke-themed dinners; and incorporated me into every social outing that she had to help get me out of the house. She helped me through such dark times back then... she'll never know how much her unconditional support meant. Lauryn even remembered to message me on Valentine's Day, post newborn and all, just to let me know that I was in her thoughts.

As Lauryn expressed her new mother woes, I felt for her to the extent that I could relate, and I wish that I could have supported her even more by really understanding what she was going through. She had had a difficult pregnancy and her new baby was waking almost every hour of every day—and for several months. Lauryn wasn't sleeping and had even begun hallucinating and, one night, scared herself when she saw a coffee table in the baby's room, which somehow vanished when she went to put her feet up on it. It wasn't until then that I really understood exactly how much our friendship had grown, from the days in college where our only priorities were ruled by boxed wine and Smirnoff Ice—to the days where sleep was, in fact, now a luxury. Lauryn, never one to study, was now reading books on parenting.

I laughed, thinking back to when she failed her driving test three times and now… she was looking up new mommy groups to join by herself.

"It's such a strange mix of emotions to be a mommy now," she said to me one day. "I didn't think that I was even capable of giving out such an intense, selfless love."

I smiled back at her. I already knew that she was a good mother. Her baby had hit the lottery with her.

"I am so full of love and busy in ways that people without kids could never imagine," she continued. "… but it's all worth it."

Zing. And there it was.

If I heard it once, I heard it a million times. I wasn't a mother. I wouldn't understand. I knew that that's not how Lauryn really meant it, and that she would never intend to dole out commentary that seemed so abrupt. But I had heard the "people without children" spiel over and over from almost every friend of mine with children and then some, including from coworkers, strangers, family, and basically everyone else— and so I was a little surprised when Lauryn said it, because she had always been extremely hypersensitive.

At the same time, I recognized now that Lauryn should feel entitled as a mother. She had earned that right. She had carried around a baby for nine months and her life would never be the same, maybe in some bad but mostly good ways. And parents have it, no doubt, 200% different than me. I can do things like… take a nap whenever I want. Sleep in. Go to my favorite restaurant. But I think when people say that "People without kids don't understand," or "You wouldn't understand," or—"Wait until you have kids," they're assuming one thing, by default:

That I don't want kids at this point in my life.

Most people, like Lauryn, mean it innocently enough. To the others who haven't meant it so nicely, I'd like to point out that I don't go around saying things like, "I love that I don't have children, because I love my expendable income." Or some other sort of generalization like, "You don't understand how busy I am at work, because I am very important and work on very important projects." Because those would be bitch things to say.

Second, the assumption in fact couldn't be further from the truth. I want kids. I want kids now. And I know that I keep emphasizing the ideal of age—but, that's also the truth: at an older age, breakups become harder, because I imagine that most people feel like they're giving up the "what ifs" of their future, which includes the near-sighted goal of children. While I understand that my life hasn't led me to having children yet, I'm still human. I still get that five seconds of zing. And I also wonder, whenever people say comments like that to me, if they're somehow right. I wonder if a mother's love is one that I'll never understand because I might not ever experience it. I wonder if I'll be able to adopt. Right now, I don't know. But the one love that everyone says that I don't understand is the one that I really, really want.

One day, I told Lauryn that I felt very isolated from my friends. I still felt very alone and I wanted children. I wanted to feel complete. Lauryn of course told me that I couldn't control and plan for everything in life, and we both knew that that was just something that she was supposed to say. But, later during the conversation, Lauryn confided that she felt very alone too. Many of her other close friends were married, but they hadn't yet begun to conceive. She felt like she had no one to talk to, either, and she was scared to raise a baby. We were both scared.

Another friend, Natalie, was one I routinely turned to with relationship woes, primarily because she had gone through a breakup and move as well, and it was around the time when I started dating Mark. I looked up to her as a role model, and I was proud of her for cutting loose old ties to pursue whole-hearted happiness. Not a lot of people get the guts to do that, and not a lot of people always think that they have the freedom to do that.

During and after her breakup, we discussed her highs and lows and insecurities with starting over, and she even turned to Mark for advice and asked him to help her move. Then, after some time went by, when she met a genuinely great guy, I was ecstatic for her. She had put some hard work into herself, and she deserved it.

About a year later, I broke up with Mark, and I thought that same level of understanding would be reciprocated, partnered with a reach out here and there. But, Natalie was busy. Busy in love. I was still happy for her, because she had prioritized what was important in life, which was herself at the time, and she made sure to pursue a healthy relationship. But when I needed help moving or packing, or needed to… just talk, even through a text or two, she was nowhere to be found.

Six months after my breakup, after my two moves and after we finally got together one evening, I filled her in on what was going on. How I still cared about what our mutual friends thought, how I was still angry… at everyone and everything. Instead of relating and offering up some sort of sympathy, which is what I had hoped for and honestly expected, she gave off a surprising air of judgment:

"Lisa, why do you still care what everyone thinks? You care too much about what people think about you."

I paused. This wasn't the girl that I used to know, the one who used to text me whenever she was single and feeling blue. She wasn't the friend that I used to

plan girl's nights with, or the one who was just so easy to talk to—about anything.

"I've always over-cared about what people think about me," I had replied at the time. "That's just who I am." I mean, I didn't know what else to say, other than the truth.

"Well—you're just better off all around. I mean, look where I am now. I'm planning three different trips with Kirk this summer, and we honestly have the best nights together, just doing nothing. We've been talking about an engagement and ring settings, like this one. Want to see?" she asked, holding up her phone.

Needless to say, after the dinner, I was caught off guard. I wasn't expecting Natalie to counter my venting, because I was honestly expecting her to welcome it… or to at least listen to it. She had been there. She knew what I was going through and what it all felt like. I was surprised by how judgmental she had become, and I couldn't shake off an odd feeling. Was it me? Was I that selfishly unhappy where I couldn't even appreciate getting together with a friend?

What kind of friend was I?

The encounter tugged at me and, when I spoke to my friend Karlie about it, she explained:

"It's not that you're a bad friend, but you're obviously going through a lot right now. Here she is, talking about engagements. A bit of sensitivity is needed. Now, Natalie's life is perfect and she feels entitled. She doesn't want to relate to you."

And then Karlie added:

"Remember, though—you used to be that, Lisa."

She was, of course, completely accurate, which forced me to scale back my irritation just a bit. Despite my ongoing and exhaustive efforts toward perfection, I'm human. I'm flawed. I'm sure I haven't reacted to certain situations like I should have—I'm either short a bunch of words or completely silent, and neither is helpful during a time of celebration or need. Now, all of a sudden and because I was vulnerable, I was wanting even more from my friends. But most of them didn't actually know how bad I was hurting, and some of them didn't even know that I had broken up with Mark. I had been so wrapped up in being with Mark that I hadn't made the time to maintain many of my friendships, and I was expecting a sudden swarm of my girlfriends to come tending to my tears. As Karlie reminded me, I too was once busy in love.

I justifiably began pulling back from some people, like Natalie, which prompted me to inventory the rest of my friends. I have always been someone who has been friends with a variety of groups, instead of with just three or four core individuals. When events like, say, my birthday rolls around, not everyone knows everyone because I'm friends with my main high school group, other high school friends, coworkers from many jobs, sorority sisters, former college classmates, neighbors, and so on. Since I had been dating Mark, I had become close with many of his friends and friends' wives, and we had also grown chummy with a lot of other couples, including our neighbors.

My first thought wondered to the mutual friends that I shared with Mark, because I felt the need to defend myself against all of his injustices. Most had heard that we had broken up, and I couldn't help but to wonder what he had told them. Had I broken up with some of them, too? I felt like a main facet of my support network was in limbo.

After several months, a few friendships did fall by the wayside, and I knew that I would miss them. I wanted to voice my side of the story, but I figured if one or two people had already made up their minds about me, then there was nothing else left to change. I kind of already knew, in the back of my mind, that that was going to happen anyways. I had also moved and was no longer within walking distance of many of my friends, and so my happy hour invites became less and less. Convenience is the commonality of many friendships, whether we want to admit it or not—just like with the friendships with our coworkers, the people we see every day. I thought back to the number of colleagues I had exchanged promises of "it'll still be the same," whenever someone got a new job. It never was. I thought about the coworkers I talked to daily before I got laid off, and I thought about how infrequent our relationships are now. I couldn't help but to anticipate even more loss, which hurt.

With the beauty of this logic also rose an embarrassing realization: I was a whiny extremist. Admittedly, yes, many of my friends were married or in long-term relationships, because that's what happens as you get older. You start to settle down, because you know more and more what you need and want. It was also natural for me to gravitate toward couples when I was in a relationship, so I was used to hanging out with that sort of crowd. It was easy to go on double dates and align myself with others in my same situation, sharing stories and sometimes venting, and just being able to relate with one another.

But why was I viewing myself as a failure? Where was my confidence?

As if I were reviewing some sort of organizational chart, I thought about my other friends who weren't in relationships. My close friend Michelle was single, my college friend Holly was dating—but no one in particular, and my neighbor had just broken off an engagement. Once I focused on the full spectrum of my friendships, I had a variety of friends surrounding me—single, married, with children, without, single parents with children, and so on. I just hadn't always turned to my single friends for relationship advice… it wasn't that I knew they wouldn't get it. I guess I just assumed that they wouldn't want to listen to it, or that they wouldn't want to join Mark and me for dinner or for a night out at the bars as the third wheel. But that was my assumption and, in retrospect, it was wrong

and I finally understood what Karlie meant. I seemed smug, because I was at the time, and I needed to be brought back down to earth. It was time for me to get humble. And so as I was readjusting to my new life, I started to find that my friendships began to adapt and evolve as well.

My one friend from college, Holly, happened to be an unexpected saving grace. I hadn't spoken to her in years, but her Facebook updates still popped up on my news-feed and she had posted that she was moving into the city, about a 20-minute walk from where I used to live.

One evening after work, I randomly texted her to see if she wanted to meet me for a happy hour. I still had her number in my phone from back in the day, and it kind of felt weird. It was out of the blue and I felt a little guilty for not having kept in touch with her. I figured that she was probably busy and would wonder what prompted my text, but she responded right away with, "Sure! Thanks for texting me!!"

When we met up, I was suddenly reminded of why I liked her so much—she greeted me in cut-off jean shorts and a T-shirt, and with her 90-pound Newfoundland lab in tow. We grabbed a seat on the patio at an outdoor pizza place and ordered plates of French fries drenched in duck fat. And when she also ordered whisky, I remembered even more why I always thought she was so bad ass. She was the perfect com-bination of female: a flirty blonde-haired, blue-eyed bombshell who could dress up and look absolutely killer, but someone who also knew how to change a flat and who carried a Taser in her purse. Even better? She never had to use her looks to get what she wanted. She is the type of person that I admire the most: a smart, hard worker.

We started out talking about her dog and her family, and the new anchor tattoo that I noticed on her foot. We reminisced about college and our jobs at the same law firm, and we talked about the city and all of the little eateries that I recommended.

"I really wish you had stayed in the city," she had said that night, motioning to the waiter for another round of drinks. "But I guess it's just my luck—I'm always a second behind! I don't really know a lot of people here yet."

"Join the club," I said, gulping down my Malbec for a fresh pour, even though I still had half of a glass left. "I miss the city, but I needed to move. I actually even moved twice." I rolled my eyes.

"Well… I wasn't going to ask, but since you brought it up… what happened with you and Mark? Are you OK? You two were together forever," Holly said.

"It felt like it, right? At least, it probably seemed that way on Facebook," I said.

"It did, and it seemed perfect," she said, swirling her fry around in barbecue sauce. "I wanted to be like you."

I half smiled. It wasn't like I was going to Instagram our fights or my bouts of stress hives. "Well, we broke up because our priorities separated, and we weren't on the same page anymore. We fought every day. Every day. It was cruel. And then we fell out of love... But I think I'm doing better now. How do you even know when you're better?"

It was a rhetorical question, and I wasn't expecting Holly to answer it. It slipped out with the momentum of my thoughts and I was embarrassed that I had just dumped my woes on her. This wasn't what I wanted. I wanted to have a carefree and fun happy hour, and I was wrecking the mood.

"After some time," she said. "It's like when you know you like someone, or even when you know you hate someone. When you know, you know."

"I just guess I can't help but to wonder how it feels to be one of those girls whose life works out perfectly," I said. I couldn't help but continue. "I wonder how it feels. Marriage. Boom. Children. Boom. Perfect career. Boom."

"Who doesn't want that?" Holly asked, picking up with hysterical laughter. "But that's not how life works. Plus, then you'd probably be a simpleton and expect everything to be handed to you."

I didn't know how to respond to her laughter, so I laughed back too. We stuffed more fries into our mouths, and then she softened. She opened up that, when I was with Mark, she had been dating a guy for more than three years.

"When he got stationed, we dated long distance and… I was going to move to California to be with him," she said. "But eventually, he stopped talking about me actually moving there... and then I started to sense him pulling away, and then we stopped speaking all together. We broke up about ten months ago. I got… I got dumped."

I stared at the ground for a little bit and then all I knew to say was, "I'm really sorry, Holly…"

"It's OK, Lisa. Really, it is. I'm doing much better than how I used to be."

"How long did it take? I mean, are you better now?"

"I mean, I'm still getting over things…" Holly said. "In the beginning, it was really rough. I'm sure you know. And sometimes I still cry, but mainly I've just been trying to focus on my new job and living down here in the city. The change is good. It's needed."

"And you like your job?"

"I kind of have to. I mean, I had to take the first one that was offered. I'd been laid off for more than a year."

I remember pausing and trying not to laugh. Not that I thought that anything was overly hysterical, but it was more of a "hah!" in the back of my throat. For some reason, I never thought that anyone could have ever related to my simultaneous low of a layoff and a breakup. But life happens to everyone. It's just funny how we always feel like we're the only ones going through tough times. I never could have imagined in my wildest dreams that Holly and I would have ever reconnected, let alone on private matters that neither of us wanted to speak about. I hadn't opened up to any of my close friends and, from the looks of it, she had kept everything inside too.

During that evening, right in that moment, Holly snapped me out of my self-pity. It's a necessary part of the healing process, don't get me wrong… but I finally realized how it felt when my life actually didn't go my way for a change, and that there was nothing that I could do. We both got that the people who look like they're leading perfect lives are the ones who are the furthest from it.

I never would have expected to become as close as I have with Holly as I am now. If I hadn't seen her Facebook status about moving, or if I hadn't randomly texted her—we most likely would have lost touch. I would have remained feeling very alone. So I'm aware now, more than ever, that friendships cycle. If you value a friendship, but feel it changing, let it fall back. Some may even disappoint you, but remember that we are all flawed human beings. We're all still learning. Some friendships, much like relationships, can unexpectedly grow intense and develop into ones that really will last forever.

Now, Holly is one of my closest friends, and she isn't someone whose friendship I'll allow to fade away again. She's a great listener, and an even better advice giver, which she so happened to dish out to me the other day. We met over plates of tater tots and sushi this time, and Holly summed everything up best: "Seriously? What are you complaining about now? Remember when you didn't have a job or a place to live? Order yourself another drink, and do us all a favor, Lisa. Just shut up."

7

Love Me Some Me-Time

Looking back, I realize that I was depressed. Maybe some part of me was in denial about it and didn't want to believe it, even though I knew that sleeping fourteen hours on the weekends wasn't normal for anyone.

And so I had no choice but to give myself the time I needed. Instead of fourteen hours, I gave myself thirteen hours to sleep in on the weekends. Months with no expectations and goals.

Eventually, I began uncoiling myself out from my comforter more and more. I fought the impulsive urges to fantasize about Mark and the "what ifs," and my emotions began to gradually level out. I continued reading my self-affirmations every day, and I began to feel better. Soon enough, I realized that I had free time when I stopped napping so much. I had a lot of free time.

Why Am I Still A Bored, Sad Blob?

Living by myself was still an adjustment, and my quiet little apartment was only interrupted by the TV or other residents thudding around overhead. I didn't have anyone to cook dinner with or mindlessly watch TV with, and I was pretty bored. The combination of being bored and sad was like the one time I accidentally took too much Tylenol and ibuprofen together, and I became this really nauseous, lethargic blob.

In fact, it was exactly like that.

I expressed this sentiment to a friend of mine, who told me that now—more than ever—was the time to indulge in "me-time" and to become completely consumed in myself.

"My therapist told me that I'd find it a welcome change if I gave it a chance," Loren said. "You know, being with myself, even though I was used to always being around another person."

She had gone through a bad breakup several years earlier and, I swear, she mentioned her therapist more than her current husband. That day, Loren was dressed in pink and had a giant pearl necklace on that was so large it resembled a Christmas sleigh bell wreath.

"But how am I supposed to enjoy being with myself, when I hate being alone because I'm always bored?" I asked, staring at Loren's acrylic nails. She reminded me of Elle out of *Legally Blonde*.

"That's easy," she said, very matter of fact. "Just like with a doctor's appointment, you need to plan ahead for and commit to appointments with yourself, and turn off your computer and put down your phone.

My therapist said to try out a whole bunch of stuff and see what sticks, even if it's just for an hour a day."

Forcing myself to spend time with myself? I laughed off the sentiment but then, after a couple of days, I figured that it was probably worth a shot. My naps were becoming less and less, which was a good thing, and I needed to fill the hours.

At first, the process wasn't easy, because I realized that I didn't actually have any personal hobbies. My old routine typically involved working and then coming home to spend time with Mark, and even then we didn't really do anything productive together. I also didn't participate in group gatherings like cooking or book clubs, either, and so I realized that I was going to need to build up this "me-time" concept from scratch.

I started by ordering books off of Amazon and reading in bed or on the couch, still in my pajamas. I've always had an affinity for actual books, the kind I can dog ear and highlight, and so my desk started to stack up quickly with everything ranging from food and travel to comedy to my favorite, nonfiction. I even jumped on the Candy Crush bandwagon, albeit about five years too late, and eventually found myself permanently stuck on level 149. (My mother, however, has beat the game and waits for software updates.)

I'm a Food Network Star

In addition to reading, I tried turning my Pinterest habit into a productive one: I actually printed out my recipe pins, went grocery shopping, and then made ridiculously time-consuming recipes. I cooked idiotic things like riced cauliflower pizza crust. I grated zucchini for far too long to bake zucchini bread for my coworkers. I fried fritters. I candied pecans in my crockpot. And, I made wonderful things like gluten-free banana pancakes topped with whipped cream for breakfast.

Food. Yum. My newfound hobby of cooking was a different routine from all of the takeout that I used to order back in the day, and I found it to be surprisingly fulfilling… and, admittedly, simultaneously time consuming.

I had also always wanted to try out food delivery services, like the kind that ships ingredients to your front door and then provides you with accompanying step-by-step instructions. The boxes were a bit on the pricey side for what I could afford, so I waited for an online deal and then I went and signed up for it. First-time subscribers were the only ones eligible for the discount, so I pretended to be three different people and ordered three boxes with three different emails, each at staggered delivery dates. Sometimes, you gotta do what you gotta do.

At first, being shipped already peeled and deveined shrimp, along with freshly peeled garlic, was luxurious. I ripped ingredient after ingredient out of vacuum-sealed pouches and followed the laminated recipe cards to make spicy chorizo stew, seared filet mignon, and sweet buttered carrots. I julienned basil and minced rosemary

on my slippery Ikea cutting boards, and I ate high on the hog. Paired with a glass of wine and my newly discovered show at the time—*Fixer Upper*—my evenings were full and I was content. I felt triumphant. I hadn't cooked a meal that I wanted to eat, and watched a show that I wanted to watch, in what felt like forever. I didn't have to do things anymore like pause over the sports channels. Instead, I flipped past them, chowed down on my mushroom caps, and became completely engrossed in demo day after demo day.

Who knew that people as nice as Joanna Gaines even existed? To this day, it's one of my personal aspirations to be as nice as Joanna, even though I know it never will and never could happen.

Anyway, niceties aside, my foodie routine went on for several weeks. Each delivery box contained three meals for two people, so I cooked and ate the portioned six meals a week. Those meals were, of course, sizeable enough that I had leftovers, so sometimes I had almost nine restaurant-style meals to be eaten within one week.

Eventually, I couldn't eat as fast as I could cook. The produce started to pile up and go bad, and I couldn't help but to feel a pang and wonder why they didn't make food delivery services for a single household containing one single person, such as myself... basically, meal kits for spinsters. And, on that note and if I were completely honest, cooking whatever I wanted to eat was fun... but also kind of lonely. I felt like my right arm was missing, because I didn't have anyone to help

me. I wanted to turn to someone to say, "Oh, this tastes good!" Or, "Should I have added more salt?" I wanted to enjoy the entire process with someone. But instead, I ate in silence and was still needing to get used to it.

My fascination with food delivery services subsequently subsided as quickly as it began but, during those three weeks, I realized that my evenings had become busy. Even though I was still incredibly anxious, I was productive. I had eagerly come home every night to cook, and it was the first time in a long time that I didn't dread coming home to my empty apartment. And, when I actually stopped moping and got out of bed on the weekends, things weren't so scary after all and it was easier to indulge in me-time.

I started enjoying the process of exploring new likes: I bought eucalyptus shampoo and stood in long, almost scalding hot showers while my scalp steamed and tingled. I continued watching the reality TV shows that I liked and decided that if I were ever on *Chopped*, I would just make a smoothie with everything. I even bought the kind of mango-mania-scent-overload soap that I always wanted to buy. To this day, I will never go back to plain hand soap again: unscented soap, definitively, is for peasants.

As even more time passed, I felt a once familiar, low guttural feeling bubble up, which was my deep goal-setting drive of mine resurfacing. Loren had been right. I was thoroughly enjoying my me-time, and the process began to tease out forgotten facets of my personality.

One morning, I randomly decided to write down what I wanted to accomplish over the next few years:

1) Write a book and get published
2) Publish my children's book manuscript with my mother
3) Launch a blog
4) Pay off my credit card
5) Buy a house
6) Lose 15 pounds

The list was pretty standard for most peoples' goals, which included improving my career, finances, and health. But when I looked at the list with a more realistic eye, I became overwhelmed. Lose weight? But I love Chipotle too much. And my debt? I had racked up some hefty numbers from my former Sunday Fundays and now with all of my moving expenses.

My self-doubt started up like a treadmill, slow and manageable at first, but then it picked up speed and became increasingly uncomfortable. *If both losing weight and paying off debt were so easy, then why were there weight-loss centers and debt consolidation firms? If I couldn't control it then, how can I control it now? And not even control things… but get ahead of them?*

My inner critic continued on to my other goals, like writing and publishing a book, which could take years, and even then be rejected by publishers. And, what about buying a house? To have to do it by myself was frightening. I could barely reprogram a thermostat as it was, let alone maintain a home.

…But what was I so afraid of?

Do They Make Pills for Self-Esteem?

If so, I should auto-purchase a monthly, lifetime supply of them. I've never honestly understood why I've always been so critical of myself, because I've worked hard for and earned most of what I've wanted in life. I'm accomplished, and I'm determined. So, I had to ask myself: what happened to the woman who once simultaneously worked a full-time job, went to graduate school full time, and also wrote as a columnist and freelancer—another full-time job?

Now, I was living my life in part-time mode, and it was time to make up for that person who I gradually let slip away. I wasn't some failure. I was just someone who needed to find a shred of dignity, otherwise known as my self-esteem.

I drove to the nearest office supply store, bought a daily planner, and then taped my list of goals in the front cover. I wanted to create a plan that was achievable, and so I broke down each long-term goal into yearly, monthly, weekly, and even daily tasks, which translated into a more realistic list. I wanted to literally see how I *could* achieve them. Here is my general, beginning outline:

1) Write a book
   a) Write fifteen hours a week out-side of the workday (~2 hours a day)
2) Publish the children's book manuscript
   a) Research agents for one hour a week on the weekend
3) Launch a blog
   a) After the book is complete—commit to fifteen hours a week
4) Pay off my credit card
   a) Establish a monthly and weekly budget
   b) Pack lunch 4x/week
   c) Take the bus to work
5) Buy a house
   a) Pay off debt
   b) Speak to an agent and lender in 12 months
   c) Determine expenses and savings (HOA fees, property taxes)
6) Lose 15 pounds
   a) Pack healthy lunch 4x/week
   b) Work out 3x/week

Clearly, this list was extensive and full of goals that I might not ever accomplish, but I quickly realized that that was the point. I wanted something drastic to change, and so I needed to set goals that could match that mentality—and, better yet, these goals could be attainable if I stuck with them in small increments.

I still wasn't entirely 100% back to my old self, but it was promising to want to be productive again and I was caught by surprise. I reminded myself that I had been in pretty bad shape. No matter what anyone else around me had gone through, even if it was exponentially worse, I personally hadn't experienced anything harder during my life than that summer. Now, I was writing goals that even the average person would be intimidated to set. This time, time was on my side, because the real me was starting to push through again.

As a writer, I obviously recommend giving the list-making route a shot, because if you want any future relationship to grow and evolve, it's important to set goals for yourself first. A lot of the time we think that a relationship should grow as a unit. But in my opinion, growth starts with each person pushing forward—kind of like the act of walking, requiring the cooperation of each foot to actually move and in the right direction. I've had moments when my stride was impaired, like the time when I fell down a flight of steps and broke my toe on my left foot. For the next few months, I walked slower and with a gimp, even though my right foot was perfectly fine.

You, of course, don't have to write extensive lists like I did, but I work best when I'm working toward long-term goals, so that's what I did. If you work best in other ways, go for it—see how you feel in setting small goals for yourself, like going a week without complaining (it's harder than you think). No matter how you choose to do it, some sort of productivity is crucial toward self-fulfillment and happiness. Don't believe me? Well, imagine how accomplished you feel after doing laundry (and let's be honest, it's not really that hard). Now imagine how accomplished you'll feel after hitting your short- and even long-term goals.

Once I established my direction, I needed to create a routine that would help me chip away at my goals. Every Sunday evening, I reviewed my list of long-term goals, even though I already knew what they were. Those two minutes were crucial—they refreshed me of my direction, like a church goer seeking holy inspiration for the week. Gradually, they became expounded into my subconscious, and I was constantly thinking about them and working toward them whenever I had free time. I tried to accomplish some small task every day toward my career, finances, and health.

Help Me, I Have Carpal Tunnel Syndrome

Similar to many writers, my day job was fulfilling, but I wrote for others to pay the bills and so the projects were never personal. In the past, I freelanced during the evenings and weekends—and the work was tedious. I've always been so attached to my computer that I have things like... orthopedic seat cushions, neck wraps, and Bengay patches and ointment to slather on my neck, arms, and wrists. Seriously, don't tell me that I'm not some sort of athlete. I've sustained a spectrum of muscle aches over the years for my commitment to the art.

This time around, though, I wanted more than binder after binder of clips. Even when I was in college, I had always wanted to write a book, like most writers dream about doing. But, I was too intimidated to commit myself to such a time consuming idea that could, as I mentioned before, end up being rejected. Still, whenever I thought about my dreams or my goals, this time to the ones that I recently wrote, the desire to write a book always remained throughout the years, and I could never scratch it off. I knew that now was the time to start, and that I'd hate myself more if I never started than if I completed a book that ended up being rejected. And, hey, even if I spent my lifetime writing something that landed in the bargain buy-out bins at a wholesale club, then so be it. At least I could tell people where to buy it.

What many people don't know about me is that writing is extremely hard for me. It doesn't come easy, and I get distracted very easily. I'm not the type of person that can lock myself up in the attic of a log cabin and write page after page of perfectly curated prose on a typewriter. That's what people think that writers do, and that it's this romantic, easy art. But that's actually the furthest from the truth—writing requires substantial time and discipline. I've had some friends not understand why I couldn't make it to their events and that's because, when I'm on a deadline, I can't just walk away from my computer, just like I can't leave the office whenever I want when a report's due. And the other problem? Writing's very easy to walk away from. I can get up to go take a nap or a shower. Or, I'll think about needing to buy matching wooden hangers for my entryway closet, so that people will think that I'm fancy. I'll think about the clothes that I've left sitting in the dryer for a week. If I leave the TV on, I'll start watching it, or I'll stare at people I don't know on Facebook. And I think that the worst part of writing is that you need a computer to do it—and with computer access comes the Internet and a wealth of distractions, like Pinterest. All you have to do is click that little Google beach ball icon, and bada bing, bada boom. You've just lost yourself two hours of critical writing time.

When I do write, and I've always done this—I silence my phone and actually flip it over, so I can't see the screen and I'm not tempted by texts or news updates. Most of the time, when I sit down to write, I don't even know what I'm going to write about. But I make myself at least sit down in front of my laptop, with my fingers on the keyboard, and I make the effort to turn off any distractions. One Friday night, I thought about what and who affected me the most during my life, and I sat down on my couch to draft a rough outline on a pad of paper. I think I only wrote down three points about my topic. Then, the very next day, I started on page one—I still didn't know the middle or the end of what I wanted to say but, every day, I wrote. Sometimes I wrote a sentence and that sentence might have taken me an hour. Other times I sat down for five hours and I felt like things were really jiving. I committed to writing every single day, even if it were to just stare at the screen on my laptop.

As a few more months went by, I looked forward to the start of each day and going to work, only so that I could come home to write some more—and for myself this time. When I finally got down to editing the last few chapters, I took vacation days off from work so I could engross myself entirely into the book.

What did I end up writing?

Well, you're reading it. I wrote this during every day of my depression. I pushed myself to do anything but sleep, and I found that I had a lot to figure out and, ultimately, to say. I had built writing into my daily mentality, which became a powerful tool. And if you're reading this, none of this would have ever happened if I hadn't decided to simply start.

Beans And Rice: It's What's For Dinner

As I spent more time writing, I was going out less with friends. Spending my nights at the bars became replaced with hours of revisions, watching TV, or cooking dinners. I also couldn't walk down the street to the nearest pub anymore—I had moved to the outskirts of the city and had to go grocery shopping or order delivery… and wait an hour even for that. Since the regular $50 a night food and bar tabs stopped accumulating, I realized how much money I had really spent—and how much I could start saving. I created a budget and went old school: I took out cash for my weekly expenses, so that I could freely spend whatever I had left over. Sometimes, that meant a $4 bottle of wine (paired with antacids) or a bottle of nail polish, because I couldn't afford the nail salon. I continued freelancing to help with the bills, I meal planned, and I took control of my finances with a strong arm. Don't get me wrong—I still missed the convenience of my friends and our city gatherings and our cookoffs, and my favorite bar with its plates of nachos and all-you-can-drink red wine specials. But now, to finally be in control of my life, well... it felt tremendously better.

One week, I even made myself eat rice and beans every night for dinner. I was mad at myself for having accumulated debt, because there was no legitimate reason for it. And so, at the cost of $10.88 with tax, I was able to buy five cans of black beans, one packet of taco seasoning, one box of brown rice, and one bag of shredded Mexican cheese. (Literally, I did the math.) That week, I ate five dinners at the price of one glass of wine, and I tucked away the money that I had saved to pay off my credit card. It sounds self-punishing, and it absolutely was.

sports and when I'm made to, I do it to engage in the social comradery of it all. And then, there's this: I was planning on leaving this part out, but whatever. Who cares? During my freshman year of high school, I was THE only girl cut from the field hockey team. I had enrolled in camps, I bought two sticks so my friends could practice with me, and I still got cut.

And so it goes without saying that I knew that this goal was going to be my toughest one yet. I can force myself to work sixteen-hour workdays, but I can't force myself to work out for one hour. But in my attempt to fling everything at the wall to see what stuck, I decided to buck up, sign up, and attend a barre class, solo. I'm not one to typically do those types of things alone and without a support system on hand, so I was particularly proud of myself. It's the small victories, right? Friends raved about the classes that have you plié and perform various barre work to tone and tighten the core and glutes, so I figured, why not? My entire body had needed tightening since 2007.

When I walked into the reception area, in a high-ceilinged, historic building in Baltimore, I was met with a familiar face, an old mutual friend, Kara. She was dressed in tight black pants and a black tank, and was pacing around, tapping on her cell phone. I naturally couldn't help but to cringe and scream silent obscenities to myself. The one class that I wanted to attend by myself would, of course, include someone that I used to know. I hadn't spoken to Kara for a while, not since

Mark and I had broken up, and I wasn't in the mood to make small talk. I figured I'd just slip quietly onto a mat at the opposite side of the room and then wave a friendly hello, like I had just seen her.

Kara's head snapped up, recognizing me instantly. "Hiiiiiiiiiiiiiiiiiiiiiiiiiiiiiiiiiiiiiii, how are you? I haven't seen you in such a long time," she gushed, walking toward me. She had always been a loud talker, and a few other girls looked up at our exchange.

At least she was friendly, I thought. I had never been super close with her and Mark was really the one who always texted her, inviting her to hang out. But things seemed fine, and I just figured that my hypersensitivity to what others thought about me was just flaring up again.

Then, all of a sudden, I saw it: Kara had a small black earpiece that hooked around her ear, which was equipped with a black foam ball, the size of a ping-pong ball, wrapping around to the front of her mouth. It was a mic. She was a newly certified barre instructor. My instructor for the next hour.

By the time class started, only four other girls showed up, and I remained standing on my mat that I had dragged to the far left corner of the room, even though everyone else clustered together near the front.

"Girls, it's a small and intimate class today," Kara said, turning up the music. "Everyone, pull your mats to the front!"

She began by instructing us to start with a small orange ball in between our legs, which we had to hold in place with our thigh muscles while we squatted with our feet in a V position. Already, my thighs began to instantly ache and it was only within the first thirty seconds. That's something else about me that I'm not the most comfortable with: I sweat profusely and—literally—like a linebacker, even if I'm exerting minimal effort when exercising. (I feel like there's a medical definition that can explain this.) Rolling beads of sweat began pouring from my hairline, and I took turns switching my arms from first position to shouldering off sweat from my forehead.

How was I doing so far? I looked around to compare my form to the others in the class, and I noted that everyone else's workout gear bore the name of the studio. These people weren't drop-ins like me. They were diehards.

Kara walked over to me with her headset on, which became amplified even more with the acoustics of the building.

"And *pulse*, 2, 3, *pulse*, 2, 3," she said, echoing.

Following her lead, we began thrusting our hips forward, still with the little orange ball squeezed in between our inner upper thighs.

"Lisa, straighten your back! And aim your hips toward the ceiling!" Kara piped two feet from behind my left ear, as she pressed the palm of her hand in between my shoulder blades.

I immediately flashed back to my first exercise pole dancing class, which was a contributing factor to why I hated group classes. The instructor had pulled me aside to an unmanned pole in the front of the room to use me as the model for poor form, demonstrating to the other girls how it's "not supposed to be done." No matter how hard I tried to correct myself, my thighs kept getting stuck and sloppily slapped around and around the pole, all while my other two friends spun weightlessly around. Whenever I sheepishly looked back to the instructor for her approval, she exasperatedly yelled, "Trust *yourself!* Let go!" I had been too uptight, and I remember leaving the class irate at myself.

The barre class followed, much to my dismay, in similar fashion as my one-time pole dancing rendezvous. I continued to maintain poor form throughout the hour, because I could barely hold the ball in between my legs—let alone stand up straight. As everyone else kept calm, cool, and collected, I quivered like an epileptic.

"Pulse, Lisa! ...2, 3... hips up, not in!"

One of the other girls to my right, who was almost six feet tall, furrowed her brows at me. "You're slowing the class down," she said. "I came here to work out!"

I gave her a sheepish half smile. She was... right. At the start of almost every set, Kara had come up to tweak my stature. I was still new to the routine and in poor form, but I kept at it and I was trying my best, even if I shrugged to Kara in the mirror with almost every mistake.

"This is my *first* class," I said through clenched teeth, suddenly changing my demeanor. "Didn't *you* start somewhere?"

My question caught the girl off guard, because she lowered her head and I knew that I was right. She did start somewhere, and she probably wasn't so good when she did.

After her comment, I made up my mind that I didn't want to care about the others in the class. Not anymore. I had paid $25 for it, and I was entitled to work out—no matter how floppy or jiggly I might be. I started laughing every time Kara sauntered over to me, and I stopped looking around at the other girls to see how deep they squatted in their pliés. By cool down, I was drenched with sweat and had had a great workout. I didn't need to make new friends at the class. I was there to work on me.

It's Time To Get Shit Done

To this day, I keep an agenda and record what I've accomplished toward my long-term goals on a daily basis, some of which are the same and some of which have changed. I wrote this book, because I spent fifteen hours a week on it, aside from my day job—and for years on end—all while believing in myself and also realizing that it may never be published.

While I haven't published my children's book yet, I recently launched a blog. I share stories from public figures. I write what I want to write about, uncensored. I have learned the nuances of blog posts, and I cry when I edit photos because I still don't understand how to do it. But I put in the work to learn one less way to fail each time.

I am also extremely committed to working on my goals even more so now. I write longer lists, I have white boards, I color code my to-dos, and I define my week by the time I can commit to whatever I need to work on.

I don't make myself eat rice and beans for weeks at a time anymore, because I've paid off my debt. And, in fact, I now take finance classes designed specifically for women with a very good high school friend of mine. I still struggle with working out and I'm not sure I'll ever feel comfortable with my physique, but it's that level of discomfort that continues to motivate me to try new workouts and to try to improve myself. Make a fool of yourself like me and maybe try a barre class, which is really like an expensive, hour-long dry humping session into the air.

No matter how you decide to set goals—set them. You're not going to be perfect every day, but the point is to try... no matter how flawed your perfectionistic self might be in each attempt. And whatever you do, for the first time in your life, take the time to be completely and 100% self-centered. Sign up for whatever you want, stop looking around at other people, and finally *do you.*

8

You *Can* Teach An Old Dog New Tricks

As I progressed even further into my new routines and toward my goals, I came to realize more and more that self-fulfillment shouldn't be paired with guilt. Transitioning to the role of a self-centered individual now took on a new meaning for me. I wasn't solely thinking of myself without giving thought to how my actions affected others. I was simply becoming more aware of myself and that heightened my sense of responsibility in being more of a kind person to other people.

I was spending more and more time alone, but I was feeling less alone than I had felt in a long time, even when I had been in a relationship. Cue Macauley Culkin in *Home Alone*—I felt like flinging open the front door and screaming, "I'm not afraid anymore! I'm not afraid anymore!"

So, I revisited asking myself: what else did *I want*?

The answer was pretty damn easy: I wanted a dog.

I grew up with dogs my entire life, and so I felt a certain void when I lived without a dog during college and while on my own. Even when I was dating Mark, it was impossible to raise a puppy or even a dog for that matter, because I commuted back and forth from Baltimore to DC every day and worked long hours. Now, I finally had the time to seek out the companionship that I had wanted for a long time—the four-footed-friend kind. Upon the recommendations of friends and, understandably so, I agreed to join the consensus of, "Adopt! Don't shop!"

I started following various Facebook pages of local animal rescue organizations. One evening, I just so happened to be mindlessly scrolling through my newsfeed and noticed that one rescue of particular interest posted a photo of a litter of six-month-old puppies rescued from a puppy mill. The rescue indicated that they were pegged by the mill as mixed designer breeds that hadn't sold, and that the mill was intending to put down the rest. Naturally, my heart slipped into a confused puddle of sheer hatred for the human race and pity for these poor animals that had, no doubt, been neglected up until this point.

I gravitated toward the photo of one apricot-colored male puppy with large round and heavy brown eyes, followed by the caption:

"Can you help me find my *fur-ever home*?"

If I could have e-signed a contract that night, I would have, but instead I set my alarm. I tossed and turned, and woke up several times, because I was admittedly intimidated by the responsibilities that came along with owning a dog: what if I needed to let him out every hour? What if he got sick? Or came with a spectrum of anxiety disorders worse than my own?

I had also always assumed that many of these firsts would be accompanied with the support of Mark—or at least another person. And I knew that I could handle the responsibilities by myself, but I didn't know if I exactly wanted to handle them by myself. But the next morning, when I woke up before my alarm with my adrenaline pumping, I knew that I had my answer. I had been learning to listen to myself a little better, and so I sped to the rescue, arriving right when it opened.

The rescue was also a feed store, and it was packed with flattened stacks of kibble and shelves of shampoo bottles and vitamins. I passed by several large crates of older dogs against one wall and, in the middle of the furthest aisle, sat a metal pen full of young dogs that still looked like puppies. They were wriggling and writhing over one another, all while freely peeing on the bedsheet tossed randomly beneath them. I reached in to pick up the lightest colored one, which I immediately recognized as the one dog from the rescue's Facebook photos.

He was about ten pounds and warm and plump, and the top of his head was covered with small, delicate ringlets. I held him with the side of his belly up against my chest, and he immediately rested his head in the crook of my neck like a tired, familiar infant.

"He's exhausted," said the owner of the rescue, approaching me. "He was in daycare this morning, running around with his brothers." She pointed to the rest of the litter, who had abruptly stopped playing and were now staring up at me. I had plucked up one of their own, and I felt like the claw out of *Toy Story*, looking down to a machine full of wondrous aliens. Every single one of them looked like they were from the Island of Misfits.

For a minute, I felt surreal. I felt out of body. I felt uncomfortable testing out a bond with an animal that I barely knew. What if we never clicked? I lifted the small dog away from my chest a couple of inches to look into his eyes, testing his reaction. As with many puppy mill rescues, his stare was unsteady and almost fearful of me. We were both uncertain of each other.

I continued to stare into the dog's eyes for almost a minute more, and then my gaze drifted to his jowls, which I couldn't believe I hadn't noticed upon first glance. He bore a severe bottom underbite that stuck out about half an inch, and he had a thick lower black lip that puckered down like a two-year old having a tantrum, exposing every single one of his tiny, crooked bottom teeth. Below that lip were about twenty or more small, black whiskers in a line, like an upside-down moustache. His front legs were bowed and misshapen, most likely from inbreeding at the mill and, while I had been holding him, his stomach grumbled with nervous farts.

The puppy felt wrong from the start. I wanted a female puppy, whose hair I could twist into barrettes. He was not what I wanted, and I reminded myself that he would be a fifteen year or so commitment. It felt like quite the decision to have to make in what seemed like a snap judgment of the appearance and temperament of an animal. Also, this dog was alarming to look at, and you could tell that he carried deep, observant thoughts behind his pooling stares. Could he tell that I thought he was ugly? That I wanted to put him back down in his pen?

All of a sudden, as we stood right by the aisle of dog beds, he flopped his head down into the nook of my neck again. I didn't know how to react, other than by smoothing the palm of my hand down his side, which felt like a fluffy down.

I contemplated the responsibilities of waking up even earlier to feed him and let him out. I was already waking up in the dark to get to work early, and my evenings were becoming busier and busier with more writing projects. And how much exactly would this dog cost me? I walked past a 30-pound bag of kibble. $39.99. A case of canned wet dog food. $25.99. Tear-free shampoo. A bed. Leash. Collar. Wire brush. The mental expenses continued to add up as I passed the rows of toys and bones.

Two long hours into my internal deliberation, still pacing up and down the aisles with the dog in my arms, a little girl in an Under Armour hoodie walked up to me, eyeing my bounty. Startled and slightly threatened, I abruptly pulled the dog's head into my chest, which caused him to go completely limp like a ragdoll out of fear.

"He's soooooo cute," she said, turning around to beckon her mother, a larger version of the pint-sized guilt trip, dressed in an almost identical sweatshirt. The little girl surpassed my armed fortress around the dog, and she touched his curls and ran her hand down his tail. Immediately, I became defensive at her definitive nature.

"I love him already," she said, looking up at me while the dog started to slide out of my arms. I didn't know what to say, so I just laughed.

"Can I hold him?" she asked.

I looked down at her and then up at her mother. "No," I said.

…there was nothing else to say.

"But, are you going to get him?" asked the little girl, who started to well up with tears. "*We* came here to get him."

"I… don't know," I honestly responded. "It's what I'm trying to figure out." The dog, who now felt like a burning ball of fire in the nook of my neck, popped up at the raised tone of my voice.

The little girl's face dropped and she went head-on to her mother's waist, wiping her tears.

I expected the mother-daughter duo to take my polite cue and leave me be, but unfortunately they didn't: forty-five minutes later, the pair continued following me and the mother approached me for a second time.

"If you're not sure if you want him, might I ask if you have another dog?"

"No," I said. "This one will be my first."

"Well, everyone should have at least two dogs. Especially since this dog is so young..." she trailed off. "He'll need a companion, you know."

"Two dogs would be very nice," I said in agreement, smiling. I knew that I didn't have to explain myself, but I continued: "But right now, I need to be sure with one. Good luck in your search for your own perfect dog, though."

I slipped into the next aisle. This was my decision to make, and I needed the space.

By the third hour of holding the dog, only letting him down to poop and pee, I knew that it was time for me to decide on the pup or to let someone else have that opportunity. He was funny looking, sure, but he had blindly trusted me for three hours, even falling asleep against me.

"I'd like to apply to adopt this dog," I said, walking to the front of the store to the owner who had first greeted me. She didn't follow a first-come, first-serve basis. Instead, she matched up temperaments of dogs to owners.

"If you want him," she said, smiling, "you can take him home today." She waved her hand toward the pile of paperwork that I had to fill out.

"Today?" I raised my eyebrows, expecting her to consider at least a few more applicants.

"Or you can take him home tomorrow. Whatever works best for you," she said. "You still have to fill out the application for our records, but if you want him, honey, he's all yours."

"Ok," I said, feeling this jittery rush start to take over me. "I'll take him today. Today makes the most sense while I'm here."

We went over feeding needs and vaccinations, and I made a neutering appointment for the following month. I picked up a leash, two bowls, a brush, and a bed. Mango shampoo, a collar, and a metal pen. Piddle pads. And after we discussed the nature of puppy mill rescues, I picked up a bottle of Resolve in anticipation of any accidents.

"Let us know what you name him, and keep in touch," one of the volunteers said, waving as I drove off in sheer terror over my new expenses and dependent. I looked down at the dog, who was now cowering in my lap. Names. I hadn't even gotten to that.

For the next hour during the drive home, I snuck peeks at the dog, who was starting to twitch as he dozed off, and when I picked him up from my lap as I pulled up to my apartment garage, he let out this soft, sleepy groan, and then pooped down the front of my sweatshirt. Pet deposit: $250. Additional monthly pet rent: $35. The costs continued popping up in little cartoon bubbles over my head as I dry heaved at the stench and hurried to my apartment.

Once inside my apartment, when I realized it was just the two of us now, this limp little creature who was covered in poo, and me, also covered in it, I couldn't help but to smile. I bent down and gently let the dog fall out of my arms and to the floor as I wiped his bottom. For a split second, I felt a pang thinking about Mark, but I just as quickly pushed the thought aside. Right now, the dog was my now, and I took one ringlet of his white and apricot curls and twisted it between my fingers.

Teddy. All of a sudden, it clicked—he reminded me of a Teddy bear, but not like the plush, expensive kind that you would find at a Department store. Instead, he was like one of those misshapen ones that had some major sewing defect at the seams, one that came out of the factory just a little too fast. Still, the way his curls framed his face and how his cowlick rested an inch or two high on the top of his head, and how the heat of his small body was comforting to hold… well, he reminded me of my old childhood Teddy bear.

"Teddy," I said, trying out his name. "I like you… I think."

Teddy began slinking around my 500-square-foot apartment, first sniffing the bottom of my couch and then the edge of my TV stand. He rolled on his back, rubbing himself like a windshield wiper against the carpeting, a soft feeling I assumed he had probably never felt before. When I fumbled for my phone to start taking pictures, he suddenly popped up on all fours, bent his back legs to a squat, and began peeing.

"Teddy, NO!"

He looked up at me as we both got used to the name. It was surprising and awkward as I said it, like an adolescent boy trying to squeak out the nerve to ask for a date.

Unfortunately, he wasn't finished: Teddy stood up, turned around in a circle, and then arched his back for a second round.

"NO!" This time, I was a little louder, but I realized that I couldn't yell at him. I picked him up instead and took him outside. Then, I ran a warm bath for him, gently massaging him all over with his new mango shampoo, until he was covered in foaming suds and my apartment smelled like a smoothie shop. I wrapped him in a blanket that I had thrown in the dryer, tucking in the corners like a swaddled baby.

"Teddy. Teddy bear. It's OK," I said, rocking him. I held him for about an hour, my little burrito bear, really tight in my arms.

That night, our first night together, Teddy eventually curled up on my pillow and wrapped his body around my head in a U-shape. I wondered if he was scared and what he was feeling, and realized how he seemed to know that I was there to protect him—unlike his previous owner. I just remember wishing that I could tell him that I wasn't going to hurt him, and just experiencing this gut-wrenching sense of guilt that I couldn't make him understand that and that only time would show him.

I immediately stepped in as Teddy's protector, but I know I verge on sounding callous when I say that I honestly didn't come to love Teddy for almost two months. It took a while for us to adjust: house training him was a specific chore, and I spent almost every hour outside with him in the dead of winter—the process took about four months, and he took a specific liking to peeing on my new sectional and on my pillow. (Rolling over in urine will wake you up really fast.) Teddy also never stopped to nap… ever. He was explosive. I was lucky enough to have the help of a dog walker while I was at work, and that helped with his energetic fits. But during the evenings and the weekends, he ran around in my apartment in circles and so often that I began to wonder if this was normal or if he had some neurological disorder. I even walked him for long walks almost every hour, for up to five to six walks a day and even more on the weekends, and I bought him every smart toy under the sun. I knew that a well exercised dog was a good dog, but I didn't understand why mine didn't have an "off" button. I eventually gave in to the assumption that he was making up for lost time and was soaking up his new life. Finally, on top of everything, one of the hardest parts was that whenever I walked Teddy, and whenever he saw another dog, he squealed and pulled his harness and leash so hard that others stared and tried to quickly walk away. His dog walker left me notes saying that "Sweet Teddy should try training lessons," and "Does Teddy know the word 'no'? He thinks he is a little king," and a handful of other residents gave me cards of trainers or recommendations of friends that they knew. But I didn't have the money for it, and so instead I just kept up at our strict routines, and I tirelessly worked with him one-on-one every evening and weekend.

One evening, after my computer took a data dump and I lost a major report, all I wanted to do was come home and go to bed. But Teddy and, rightfully so, was eager for his walks. This evening, after our first one, I sat down in the lobby of the building across from another woman recently diagnosed with multiple sclerosis. She could tell that something was wrong, and so I ditched the introductory pleasantries and opened with: "I just got my dog, and sometimes I look at him like, 'What did I do?' Is it wrong that I feel like I want to return him tonight?"

I couldn't really admit this to my friends with children; they'd think I was insane, because they had their hands even more full. I could, at any time, put Teddy in a crate and go find myself some peace and quiet. But that wasn't fair to him, and so I wasn't going to do that. Instead, I was going to play with and train him for the rest of the evening. I just felt exhausted.

The woman responded to my remark by laughing, and I expected her to give some sort of motivational speech and a, "Just wait until you have children." But she said, "That's exactly what I asked myself throughout the nine months of my pregnancy, and even on the first night I brought my son home. And he was my first born!"

I looked up at her, shocked, and then we both erupted with laughter.

"If it makes you feel better, I'm sitting here in the lobby, because I needed to get away from my husband," she added. And I smiled—and I never do this, because I'm not an overly touchy feely type of person, but I hugged her before I went back to my apartment with Teddy in tow.

"Thank you so, so much for that," I said, blinking just a little bit more than normal to cover up my tears.

As I adjusted, knowing that I wasn't alone, things just clicked after a while. My love for Teddy continually grew and, one morning when he was curled up on my chest, I became suddenly very aware of how much I loved him. I had introduced him to the sun and the grass—which was a heartbreaking but really wonderful first for me to share with him. I broke up small pieces of treats so that he could chew them, because he had a hard time eating from his dental deformities. And when he curled the edge of his paw around a ball for the first time, and started squealing over it, I became infinitely thankful for him. Teddy stopped becoming afraid of the wind every time it blew, and I stopped being afraid to take care of him.

To this very day, I'm learning a lot as a first-time solo pet owner. Like, that dogs barf a lot, and that if you leave them with a friend while you're on a week-long vacation, they'll get really mad and pee all over your bed when you come home. I also learned that dogs can become emotionally attached to toys and fall asleep cooing over their favorite brown ball that looks like a potato. That they don't understand what you're doing behind a glass shower door and will drop toys on the ledge, bribing you to come back out. And, that you can spend several minutes looking for a dog who's been silently following at your heels the whole time. Best of all, I learned that one of the greatest feelings after a long day is the warmth of a dog draping himself across your lap, the warmth of a dog who waited all day for you to come home because you're his highlight. I no longer had an empty apartment. I'm still learning, like learning how my dog will pretend he's sleeping until you leave the room—and then sneak sips of wine from my wine glass, returning back to his same sleeping position once I re-enter. My disciplinary skills have continued to lack, and I am the sheepish but proud owner of an affectionate and really rotten pup. I give Teddy bottled water when I drink tap, and he loves grass-fed lamb. He loves getting little paw massages at night, and he carries a different toy with him to bed. While this is all a little embarrassing to admit, I now understand that all dog owners go through this, much like parents do… it's a quite complex fawning and adoration process. It's also really scary to take care of a dog, a living thing who loves you—but can't talk during his whole lifetime, and whose life should be eight times longer than it really is. And the love from a dog? Well, Teddy's love for me is the kind where I can accidentally clock him on the head with the corner of my dresser drawer, causing him to yelp and get really confused for a second. But then he goes back to loving me five seconds later, curling up at my feet and bumping my ankles with his nose. I can't think of one human being who would be so forgiving. That's a special kind of love. That's a dog's love.

Sometimes in life, you make really bad and really, really good decisions, and you deal with or reap the rewards of those consequences. Was I meant to stumble across that Facebook post of misfit puppies? Was it really that random? I don't know. Either way, I'm grateful that I listened to myself and set my alarm to get up early that one Saturday morning, because I was meant to be Teddy's beta all along.

9

Just Roll With It—The Ebb and The Flow

Despite you becoming happier and healthier, there will still be those ebbs and flows that threaten your progress. There's an unpredictability to it all—that one really good day followed by the kind of day where you call out of work to watch repeats of *Hoarders* and start to envy their lives because you think they've got it so much better.

My decision to alter my schedule to focus on myself was not an easy one. I could have lived for free with friends, booked back-to-back lunch dates and bar rendezvous, and planned it so that I was never alone. But I couldn't heal by keeping busy, because then I would have just become a—very busy—sad and lonely person. I needed to fix myself first.

Once I did commit to myself, I began picking up national gigs because I finally believed in what I had to say, and I said it with confidence. On the weekends, watching a movie and cuddling up with Teddy was the buttercream icing on top of the cake. And, when I met up with my friends and family, I didn't require them to lift me back up. I didn't need to vent or talk about what was bothering me anymore. (And let me tell you, everyone was thankful for that.) I was starting to fulfill my own happiness.

Many people often ask me how long it took for me to heal and how long I think it'll take them, because people want to know when and how quickly they'll be back to their old selves. And as generic as it sounds, the truth is that that's a hard question to answer: it depends on you, the former relationship, and work you're willing to put in. And probably the most important question that I ask is: Do you really want your old self even back?

I'll of course still have days when I want to slam down my phone when everyone's bursts of happiness light up my newsfeed. But I also know that, now more than ever, I'm finally the happiest and best version of myself—even if it's just me right now.

Sometimes I think about the people who will never find out who they are or what makes them happy. That, to me, is scarier than a breakup, than being single. And, I refuse to look around one day and see that everything has fallen into place, only to realize that I've hated and complained about my life and its transitions the entire time.

What if we can work to create a life that's less motion-driven, less mile-marker driven, and instead work toward defining our own version of happiness? It's possible. I feel incredibly lucky that I've given myself that chance, and when I think of a future with someone else, I want to wait for the type of bond—slowly, through dating, a relationship, maybe even marriage—that some of my friends have. One that teases out all of the best facets of myself and equally supports all of my ugliness. I want to wait for my best friend, and that will take time and growth on both of our parts. My message isn't a plea for marriage, and I'm not here to scare off potential suitors. My message is, in fact, a push back against the immediate societal expectations and mile markers that are shoved down women's throats every day, rushing us to an ideal and not a connection. Needless to say, on the other end of the spectrum, many of my happiest friends are ones who have gone through divorces. We all draw boundaries and recognize what we want or who we want to be at different, revolving times in our lives.

As your good days increase, the ebbs, the deepest blue of the spectrum of your emotions… they'll still get you, and that's part of the process. That's life. One of the most important concepts to note, however, is that your ebbs do not mean that you are any less happy. No matter how happy I had become, I still experienced the inevitable days when I was afraid to be alone with myself and they seemed to bubble up out of nowhere. Those times were normally during the weekend or late at night, the moments when people crave company and affection and the loneliest feel it the most. I often sat on my couch and looked around at my apartment in sheer amazement whenever those days hit. I never knew that the loss of Mark would prompt my inner strength, because I had always assumed he would be the one to bring it out in me.

Even though I was proud of myself for moving on, I still missed the emotional connection that had taken years to build. Teddy slept on my pillow and, on some nights, I found myself waking up from his hot breath on my neck, thinking he was Mark. Whenever that happened, I always saw Mark's birthmark and the outline of his frame, even though it was pitch black in my room and he was never really there. I missed tickling his side whenever he snored, right underneath of his arm, so that he would snort and wake up. But I had finally stopped missing all of him.

I learned to adapt to the other aspects of my life by taking my pickle jars to work for my coworkers to open them for me. And while it doesn't make it any less uncomfortable, I got used to the question, "Are you dating anyone?" The funny thing is, the people who prickled the most at being asked when they were planning on having kids were the ones who always asked me this, and who most often asked me in public settings. I'll never forget, to my horror, someone asking me this very question at someone's kid's birthday, and the whole room going silent. But life carried on, and after that I had to work up the nerve to go to cookouts and other functions by myself, and realized that it was OK to sit in the corner if I didn't have anyone to talk to. It was also OK to strike up a random conversation. Sometimes, I got sad, because no one told me that the private and the public solitude of both a breakup and being single are very different but difficult aspects of life.

We're brainwashed to feel that if we're not experiencing an explosive high on life that something is wrong with us, and I attribute that to the highlight reels that we call social media. Feeling blue? Have a bad day at work? Then dull it with a bottle of celebrity-inspired wine or discount drinks at happy hour. Feeling anxious? Well, that's why there's pills for that. And foot wraps and essential oils. It's like society makes us believe that there is something wrong with being sad. My lingering question though is, why *wouldn't* you be sad after a long-term breakup? Why isn't that OK?

This all leads me to wonder why we're so prone to avoiding our natural emotions. So long as moments of sadness don't translate to short- and long-term depression or other mental conditions, impeding an overall quality of life, how could we truly have proper growth without pitfalls and the emotions that come with them? Even Disney and Pixar movies have conflict because that little fish with the bad fin or the overweight Asian kid become stronger because of it.

And so I say this: challenge yourself to be alone with your feelings. While you're alone, value your internal dialogue as you would during a conversation with a friend. What advice would you give to yourself? Also, much like you wouldn't dismiss a close friend when they're telling you about their most vulnerable times, don't dull your own emotions. Experience them. Learn from them. Figure out what routine helps you to work your way through the resentment, the sadness, or the loneliness—that's how you're going to fully heal.

Advice to myself, in retrospect, would have been to let go of what others thought about me. It's easier said than done, yes, and females have a special burden to bear. Visit a sorority house bathroom, versus a frat house bathroom—and you'll understand why at an exponential rate. Females are taught about the notions and potions of grooming at a young age, implying that we should care how we present ourselves to the world and that, on a more detrimental stance, we should care what people think of us in return. Simply peruse the shower gels, exfoliants, $30 eyeshadow pots, brushes, eyebrow gels, bionic blowdryers, tanning sprays, cellulite-reducing lotions, angled brushes for contouring… and so, so much more. Did you know that there are even designer tweezers and nail clippers? Yes, those are things. Males, on the other hand, have some bottles of body washes and shampoos, and that's it in their bathrooms, besides the smell of mildew.

This societal requirement to maintain the perception of our appearances is in large part as to why, when you gather females together, we compare. We sell detox teas and wraps and nail stickers to strangers on Facebook to compensate for what we feel that we lack. Our need to compare—and even to compete with one another—is innate. It's superficial. I often hear how females, my friends included, aspire to look like so-and-so or want to dress like someone else. But I rarely hear friends say how they want to also embody someone else's ideals, or her personality; that's not to say that I have shallow friends (I don't), but they're simply continuing a habitual behavior. And so I propose to change that norm, too: let's work to treat each other with a little bit more respect, even if it's just a friendly hello to a stranger on the street.

From time to time, I do have to check myself, but I've been fortunate to receive gentle nudges to practice being a better person and exactly when I need them. Almost a year later and as I continued with my routine of cooking, I decided to overcome my fear of using a gas grill. Back in the day, my first experience with a gas stove in my very first apartment had been terrifying. Thinking that the burner would warm up and *then* ignite, I had turned on and let the gas run for about fifteen minutes. (My roommate, who had a habit of lighting his cigarette inside—before actually stepping outside—nearly lost his mind on me.)

Anyways, barbecuing had always been a nostalgic summer routine for me, with Mark bulk ordering specialty barbecue sauces and me boiling sweet Maryland corn in milk and sugar for fresh succotash. This time, I was hell bent on making my own nostalgic memories: I bought chicken breasts and barbecue sauce, ventured out to the courtyard of my apartment building, and tied Teddy to a chair. But when I plopped the chicken on the grate of the grill and turned on all of the knobs, even to max, nothing happened. I closed the top of the grill but, five minutes later, the chicken was still raw.

All of a sudden, a woman yelled down to me from her balcony, "You need to turn the red handle underneath of the grill—to turn on the propane. The same thing happened to me!"

I remember looking up at her, embarrassed but still smiling big, and thanking her. She could have kept to herself and watched me leave with raw chicken because the grill wouldn't start, and I probably would have slipped into some funk for the rest of the day. Instead, she shouted down to me, and she had no idea how big of a moment it was for me to try to grill chicken on my own.

I sure did grill, too. After turning the red handle, a gush of flames barreled up from the belly of the grill at maximum power. I had forgotten to switch the knobs back off before igniting the propane. (I tried not to think about what could have happened if someone had actually been standing over the grill.) For the next two days, I ate overcooked, rubbery chicken that I dunked in barbecue sauce. It was the best damn chicken that I had ever eaten, because I grilled it.

This all brings me to my final point of the chapter: if you're reading this, and you've gotten this far, and you're married to your best friend and have kids—well, you're probably one of my family members or friends, and I probably made you buy this book. (Why would you be reading this, otherwise?) But if by chance you're not, and you're thinking, "I'm so glad this isn't me. I'm so glad I don't have to be single and go through this anymore, and I'm happy that I've found the person who completes me," then you haven't gotten what I've really been decisively pointing to the whole time, which is this: no matter who you are, or what you're blessed with—well, life can throw you some really, really ugly shit.

There's cancer, and sudden heart attacks and deaths, and things like losing your newborn's mother right before the holidays. That actually happened to a friend of mine. There's a lot worse stuff out there than a breakup and needing to get over one, and wanting to find a partner. But no matter what we've been through, and without comparing what we've each been through, how do we move through the ebbs and flows of this thing we call life?

My most definitive answer to this is to stop asking "when." We all want to know "when." When will we get over this? When will we finally become that perfect, happy person? When will this diet work and when will we be able to shed those thirty pounds? If we set our foresight on attaining that life full of continuous, perfect highs—without the steps in place, we will always fall short of our own expectations. Life is not perfect and it's full of all sorts of moments. That's why, this time around, I promised myself that I would take control of my life in an honest, realistic way—with the end goal being to give it my all, ride the ride, and ultimately… let go.

10

To Toss or to Keep?

I caught up on and learned a lot about friendships over the course of the year. I learned that Caitlin's husband almost died and that another friend was having difficulties conceiving. I learned that my friend Kevin had moved in with his boyfriend and was the proud stepfather to two small dogs, and that another friend, Allie, was recently promoted to head nurse of her unit.

I also began spending more time with Lauryn, who was adapting to and thoroughly loving motherhood. Once I took the time to heal, she and I became much closer after my breakup, because she was a good friend who knew that I needed to grow as someone else. I never owed her anything, and she never once reminded me that I hadn't been the greatest friend to her. One year, I missed Lauryn's birthday. Another year, she told me how distanced she felt from me and that she was worried that our friendship was fading. She was right, too, because I hadn't been making an effort on my end. But even though I had been a terrible friend in many ways, Lauryn stuck with me and supported me during our whole friendship—with no questions asked.

I realized that I needed to reprioritize my friendships to make time for the people who really mattered, like Lauryn. I began to shift my friendships around, similar to how I organize my files on my computer: I keep my most important files in a shortcut folder on my desktop, so that they're front and center, and easily accessible. I keep the rest of the files that I don't access as much stored in a tucked away folder, because I don't want to clutter my desktop and become distracted from what's most important.

Once I reevaluated the people who were my best friends—and not just the ones of convenience—I realized that I hadn't spoken to many of my good friends in a while, and I was embarrassed. I guess I had always assumed that they were and always would be in my corner, but that's the wrong sentiment. Friendships take work… just like with any relationship. And, I knew that I had some work to do.

I started contacting my old friends—much like with my friend Holly—to reconnect. And when I say reconnecting, I mean legitimately calling friends or pinning down a specific date to get together through text. I didn't want to pawn off a generic, "Let me know when you're free," and have that go back and forth for the next year or two. I seriously meant it this time, and the process was quick and as simple as that. I didn't take blame or feel solely guilty for not catching up on a more frequent basis, because it takes two to tango. I just took thirty seconds to make a phone call, and it was relatively easy to pick up where I left off in many friendships. Years before, I probably would have caught up with friends over rounds of drinks—and, I did with some. With others, I caught up outside at a Panera, so that my friends could bring their kids, and so that I could bring my dog in tow. Some get togethers were planned around naptimes, and other evenings out had to be cancelled abruptly if a babysitter didn't come. But life happens, and it was all well worth it.

Naturally, I started having less and less time for others, and that was OK. Yes, it would have been easier to get together with friends who lived closer and with friends who were friends out of simple convenience, but I stuck to my guns and continued to put in the work. I certainly wasn't writing anyone off, but I was becoming more conscious of my time. Life also began to take its course: some of my friendships began to naturally dissipate on their own. Others, like with Natalie who was busy in love, paused on their own.

I've always had a decent number of friends, which means that I'm constantly invited to different celebrations and things almost every other weekend—and I've never minded it. But as my friendships increasingly spoke for themselves, I began to do the unthinkable: I declined to attend if I hadn't spoken to or seen that person in three to five years. If I did receive an invite from someone I hadn't spoken to in a while—I sent a small gift. I was flattered, and it was still nice to be in their thoughts. On a handful of occasions, I sent a card—and for some, I simply just RSVP'ed a polite no.

To the majority of the rest of you, my friends, my true friends—you know who you are—the ones whose weddings or baby's first birthday that I'm helping out with, but the ones who still take the time to say, "How are you?"

Thank you.

Thank you for understanding that no matter the life stage, everyone, including me, has moments that are important. Whether it's a first step down the aisle or my transition into the first apartment of my own, all moments in life are significant. They're all encouraging growth. To my friends, thank you for calling me and bringing over wine. Thank you for understanding that I couldn't send out invitations to specify a save-the-date: join me as I cry until I get hives because I got laid off today. Hold my hand at 7 p.m. this Tuesday, because my relationship has just ended and we're splitting up our freezer mugs. Thanks for being there for me— because you understand that the difficult moments are obligatory to show up to, too. Thanks for understanding that a breakup still stings.

On top of thanking everyone and speaking from experience, it's also important to remember that friendships aren't perfect. I've always idealized that one perfect friend who encompasses everything, like the sweet listener and the snarky advice giver, the reliable happy hour goer and the grounded individual who knows how to manage money and invest. The single friend who sympathizes with my dating woes and the married friend who dishes out advice. The friend who will spend hours with me, watching Netflix, and the one who will sign up with me to try aerial yoga. But to even list these traits exhibits polar opposites and extremes, and shows that those perfect components within one person do not exist. It's one of the reasons why we have to value and nurture a variety of friendships to create a strong, rounded support system.

Finally, friendships require forgiveness, especially as we're almost always transitioning through one phase in life or another. Don't let meaningful relationships slip away—I'd be one lost pup if I didn't have Lauryn in my life today. Take the time to hold on to those quality human beings, and let's all resolve to put in some extra effort: flag your important friendships, visit them as often as you can, and keep the most important ones in your main perspective.

11

Freaks and Jerks

I wasn't ready to date when I first started dating again, which was only a few months post breakup. I obviously didn't realize this until I had already begun and, while out on dates, I found myself wishing that I were alone and back at my apartment.

"Dating is so annoying," said my friend Matthew. "It's because you're starting from square one with everyone out there."

He was so right. I was impatient that I couldn't leap to the comfortable stages where I could, at the very least, trust someone. I was also scared that the only available men out there were freaks and jerks. What if someone murdered me? The possibilities were endless.

Dating was also hard for me because I am a naturally awkward person. I'm an articulate public speaker and I'm great in front of the camera, but I can also be quiet—which is not to be mistaken for shy. Sometimes people think that I'm snobby. Sometimes they think I'm standoffish. Maybe even judgmental. When my parents dropped me off for college, in fact, their advice was: "Please be friendly and make an effort, Lisa. You're not always Little Miss Welcome Committee." And they were right, too… although, my behavioral output isn't always my intention. Beyond all of my awkward fidgeting and stares, I really am a nice person.

Two of my close girlfriends, who were also single at the time, had very different perspectives toward dating, and I fluctuated back and forth between them, depending on my mood.

Christy was my hopeful, eternally optimistic friend. I hated going to the pool with her, because she had a ripped six-pack and she was a tall, very blonde, very pretty model. She was also bouncy. Like, always exercising and going on paddleboard yoga types of excursions, and she was an enthusiastic lover of alliteration. That type of bouncy. Her optimism was infectious, and we frequently shared our thoughts on finding love.

"I was at the farmer's market the other day," she said to me one evening at a luau-themed party. "And I'm like, could this be where I meet my future husband? Could you finally be him?"

I laughed. "You mean, by the red potatoes? Fingering the farm-fresh onions?"

She smiled, used to my sarcastic banter. "Exactly. But then I looked down and he had a ring on, and I was like, 'Oh my geezy, next!'"

Like Christy, I was starting with the onset of the "What-Now-What-Next Mentality." I thought of the

P. D. Eastman book, *Are You My Mother?* Just like with the confused fledgling, that same disorienting, hopeful mentality followed me whenever I was out in public, like that time when I made eye contact with a man in my building and I overanalyzed it to be more than a simple hello.

Could you be my husband?

But then I looked down to his left hand to find a wedding ring, and then his wife came trailing behind him with the groceries.

Another time, when I was on a writing assignment, I casted stares to a suited-up man in an elevator.

Are you my husband?

But then the small talk during the ride up faded to blank stares at our own mirrored reflections.

Fine then. ***Anybody?***

I also carried this desperate optimism with me whenever I went on dates. But, after only a month or two, I always found that the chemistry faded away. I felt like there were no intermediate grounds with getting to know someone—either the guys I dated were distant and confusing (read: emotionally unavailable), or over-the-top over-communicative.

This all led me to wonder: was something wrong with me? Am I unlikeable? Why was dating so hard, particularly after the age of 30?

I have the answer to only one question right now, which happens to be the last: when you're older, when you're nearing 30, at 30, or over 30 years of age—people know what they want. And I know that I keep empha-sizing age, but it's the truth. When you have time, more time to live, learn, and experience… *everything*—people subsequently know *who* they want. And, what makes things even more complicated is that we have less time to give. We have less time to date. Even worse? Dating has suddenly transitioned to becoming not so much about fun, but more about long-term possibilities.

So what is dating like? Are you feeling lonely and awkward, too, or is that just me? Well, to help ease your pain (if you have any), the following are samples and excerpts from actual dates of mine.

1. The Shrieking Helium Inhaler

Needled by the encouragement of a friend of mine, I reluctantly went out on a blind date with one of her friends, who was (funny enough) a relationship coun-selor. She showed me his picture, vouched for him and his man bun (fine, I secretly like them), and gave my number to him. He and I both texted back and forth for a bit, and he seemed smart and witty. When we agreed to meet up, he set a date for a walk in a nearby botanical garden and then suggested lunch after. I was surprised by the thoughtfulness of his plans, and he seemed like a breath of fresh air.

When we first set our sights on each other, everything about him seemed normal—that is, until he leaned in for a hug by one of the rosebushes, and then actually spoke.

"Lisa, it is really nice to meet you," he said… in a high pitched, shrieking squeal. At the time, I couldn't even think of a cartoon character equivalent; I just stood perfectly still and in shock as other people turned to stare at the source of the piercing screams.

My friend told me that she "thought it would be good for me to finally meet a nice guy," and that she thought "I should give him a chance." Later, she admitted that she "owed me a drink."

Takeaway: He really was probably a very nice guy, and some other lucky lady will have the privilege of finding that out.

2. The Taco Eating Concert Goer

I agreed to go out with a friend of a friend, Brad (whose voice I confirmed was normal), and we met up at a taco shop. It was this small authentic place, and you wouldn't have known it from the outside of the building, which was plain and looked like a post office—the best kind of restaurants, if you ask me.

Once I walked inside, Brad immediately grabbed my hands before we could exchange an introduction. "Let me order for you," he said. "Trust me."

Caught off guard, I agreed and sat down in one of the booths and, ten minutes later, Brad came back carrying three Styrofoam plates, each with one small taco to split.

"I assume you come here a lot?" I asked as he sat down. "It's a nice change of pace."

But instead of replying, Brad motioned to the tacos laid out on the table. "Before we begin eating, let me explain these tacos to you. I like to think of these three tacos as the most recent concerts I attended last summer: Fall Out Boy, Beyoncé and Jay Z, and Linkin Park."

I poked my fork over top one of the shrimp, ready to dig in, but Brad slapped my hand out of the way. I was slightly taken aback, but more so hungry, and so I paused...

"No, no, no, Lisa," he said, "we have to eat the beef one first. This is the Fall Out Boy concert. This was my first concert." He cut the beef taco in half. "It's good, right?" he asked. "Just like Fall Out Boy."

It was *really* good, and I tried to recall some Fall Out Boy songs. But before I had time to answer, Brad was already moving on.

"Now, for the second taco," he said. "This is like the Beyoncé and Jay-Z concert. Better than Fall Out Boy, but not the best. And it's lamb. Do you like lamb?"

I paused. Forty-five minutes into the date, I was surprised that this was the first genuine, personal question that Brad was asking me. I thought I liked him. Well... I really, really wanted to like him. But something didn't feel right.

"I've never been the biggest fan of lamb, but I'll try it again," I said. "Did you like the concert? What was your favorite song?"

I tried to channel Christy's optimism. Maybe Brad was nervous. Maybe I needed to give him more of a chance and be admittedly a touch less judgmental—after all, I had my flaws right and left. I looked at him a little more closely with a little more hope. Could he be—at least—a potential? I obliged by spearing a fat strip of lamb with my fork.

"That's good. That's really good of you," Brad said, nodding his head and pulling down on his T shirt. "I hate girls who can't try new things. I once went on this first date with a girl who refused to try a bite of my sushi... and we were at a sushi place! It was such a turnoff. I literally had to force feed her a forkful of salmon and roe, and then she spit it out on the corner of her plate."

"Well, maybe she didn't like sushi," I said, rolling the lamb over my tongue and confirming that I didn't like lamb. I wanted to spit it out, but I couldn't... not now.

"Nonsense! Everyone likes sushi, just like with shrimp, which we've happened to save for last. This is the Linkin Park of all of the tacos, the crème de la crème of my concerts, the one that trumped Fall Out Boy and Beyoncé and Jay-Z," he declared.

I tried to stifle my laughter... he was entertaining, to say the least, and it was what I had wanted to eat all along. But instead of pushing my half of the taco onto my plate, Brad held up the plate between us for just a second longer, and spun it on his index finger like a frisbee to build up the most climatic moment.

Then, he pushed my half of the taco onto my plate.

"So, do you like it?" he asked.

"I do, I like this shrimp taco, this is great, thank you," I said, still on my first bite. I was starting to feel a little bit overwhelmed.

"But—do you like *this one* the very best?"

I paused. Should I be honest? Or play along and agree that Linkin Park was the best one? I didn't know what to do. "Well…," I said slowly, trying to gauge Brad's reaction, "If you want me to be really honest, I liked the beef one the best."

He sharply inhaled, as if I had directly insulted him, and then rolled his eyes. "Fall Out Boy over Linkin Park? No way, Lisa. Just no way!"

"I'm so sorry…" I gave a nervous giggle and shrugged my shoulders. I appreciated his efforts, but I was still a little bit hungry. I was going to have to stop at Noodles & Co. on the way home for some carryout.

"Well, I'm glad you're at least into trying new foods," he repeated and said, almost verbatim: "There was this one girl that I went on a date with, and I couldn't bring myself to ask her on a second date because she wouldn't try sushi. I literally had to force feed her a forkful of salmon and roe. And then she didn't like it and spit it out on the side of her plate."

By this time, I let some of my laughter escape. I almost felt bad for the guy because he was trying very hard to impress me, and dating—absolutely—can be nerve wracking. But the disconnection that I was feeling was just that—that he was extremely scripted, so there wasn't even a chance for us to even chat and get to know each other. He was so… well practiced. I realized that after the entire dinner, even though he was very nice, I barely knew anything about him.

Why can't we all just relax a little and be ourselves? It's the honest way of getting to know each other and understand if we actually *want* to get to know that person, versus wanting mere, generic companionship.

That night, near 11 p.m., Brad texted me: "I had a great time with you. We should do it again."

And the next morning, at 7:45 a.m., I got another text: "I had a really great time last night. Do you want to go out again soon? Maybe tomorrow night?"

But by that time, I had made up my mind, and I politely declined. He was overwhelming and we were not on the same page. I was just tentatively stepping back into the dating pool. We continued to text back and forth a little bit, and then we both agreed that it had been fun while it lasted—and I thanked him for asking me out. I honestly did feel tremendously guilty for turning him down, but I didn't want to go on another date with Brad… and I needed to be honest. I couldn't be a jerk and leave him hanging.

Takeway: Sometimes there's just not chemistry—and it's respectful to be a decent human being and admit it, so we can all move on. (This works both ways.)

3. The Married Man

One morning, I was visiting a local coffee shop when I was on a writing assignment. I had my laptop out, and I was actually in the groove and furiously typing. An attractive guy walked up to me, commented on the quickness of my typing, and then sat down for a brief five- to ten-minute chat. When all was said and done, he said that I looked "very pretty" that morning and in a non-creepy way, and then we exchanged numbers.

We weren't able to meet up for about three weeks or so, because we each had other commitments. During that time, we texted each other almost daily, and I thought to myself, maybe this is the nice, stable guy with good credit that I have been waiting for all of my life. Could he be a unicorn? When we finally met up, we grabbed a casual lunch and then went through the standard series of Qs & As:

- What do you do for a living?
- Do you like it?
- Where do you live?
- So what did you do this weekend?
- Have you gone on any trips recently?

- Do you have decent enough credit, so I know that you're a responsible person?*
- Do you have any dependencies on alcohol and drugs?*

*Fine, I don't ask the last two, but I anxiously hope that the answer is yes, and then no. In that order.

Then, when I also asked if he lived with roommates or by himself, he answered:

"Oh, I live with my wife."

Takeaway: It is more than acceptable to: ask for the check and a to-go box immediately (in that instance, who cares? I'm finishing up what I paid for by myself), and then leave a person in the middle of a date. Being safe is always better than being polite.

It was always after these sorts of bad dates that I called Michelle. She was on the extreme and opposite spectrum from Christy, and was the "realist," or so she said. Sometimes, she verged on pessimism. But mostly, she was snarky and spot on, and I needed her insight, especially when dating and dealing with the spectrum of accompanying characters.

"Besides the cheater, should I be giving these guys more of a chance?" I asked Michelle one day.

"Look, Lisa—I'm all about first and second dates, and really listening to the feelings that you get from them," Michelle said. "First impressions really are everything. You listened to your gut, and your instincts told you that they weren't for you. So stop seconding guessing yourself. Seriously!"

"But maybe I should give people more of a chance," I said.

"You did. It's called a first and second date. And if you're worried about being too judgmental, you're right. You're judgmental. We're all too judgmental. Give me someone who isn't and they deserve the Nobel Prize. And frankly, I get tired of the natural assumption of 'he's single, and you're single, so you should both just not be single anymore and get together.'"

"You're right… you're absolutely right," I said, relieved that I had confided in Michelle, and that she had said exactly what I wanted to hear.

Michelle continued: "I know I am. And, while we're opening up that can of worms, I'm tired of getting asked by married people, 'Who are you dating?' It's just as personal as, 'Are you trying for kids?' If I want to talk about it, I will. I feel like it's always asked by the people who don't really know me… otherwise they wouldn't ask. And, on top of that, I feel like the people who do ask are the ones who are always complaining about being asked when *they're* having kids. Double standard, maybe?"

Admittedly, at times I wanted to pull back from dating all together, but I kept at it because I had never quit anything in life, except for that evening telemarketing job in college. Was I trying hard enough? Was I too comfortable at being single? I knew that I had to keep on keeping on, because I literally had nothing to lose and I didn't want to fall into some stagnant zone of emotional safety. I needed to put myself out there, even if it meant getting hurt.

As I kept at it and almost a year later, I had gone out with a bunch of different men—all relatively decent guys (except for that one), but none panning out and lasting for more than a month or two. Then, all of a sudden, I got my breath of fresh air: I went out on three dates with Eddie, a guy I met at a cookout and who made a lasting impression on me. He owned his own house and boat, and he had a great job that he worked hard at. We also had a ton of mutual friends.

But by the fourth date, it was me who got rejected.

"Are we still on for today? Lunch maybe?" I texted. I was excited to see him again. The last time we met, we talked about work over a charcuterie plate, when it in fact turned out that we both had wanted to chow down on the house special, a burger and fries. He made me nervous in a good way, and—I admit—I wanted to impress him. I didn't get that feeling often, so I paid attention to it.

But that day, the tables turned and all I got back was: "Oh, I forgot about lunch today."

And in dating code, I knew what that meant.

"I'm disappointed," I told my cousin Kim over the phone that following week. "Nothing is working out! I'm annoyed and I'm going to die alone."

"Hon, you've just got to keep trying. I'm back in the dating realm—after having been married for sixteen years. Sixteen years! I had a truly happy, loving marriage, and I didn't date for years and years after Will and I divorced," Kim said. "This might sound silly, but you just need to try to have fun. At least open yourself up to it. Dating is one night out, one step at a time. Go have a glass of wine! Go laugh! If you want, I can sit at a table or two behind you if you're feeling uncomfortable."

I smiled, wanting to hug her.

"You're right, Kim. It is just a night out…"

I was relieved that I had called her and realized how helpful it was to talk out my worries. I was also surprised how quickly she was able to help me reshift my perspective, and I was really thankful.

"Go have fun, and just go have a laugh!" she reminded me once more.

And so—I did. I listened to her advice, because we all need advice from time to time. I laughed when a first date with an attorney did not go well, particularly when he pulled up an article of mine online and pointed out all of my errors. Another time, I had to take Teddy with me to an outside patio of a restaurant, and he began snoring and growling in his sleep. And on yet another, my very nice date ordered a grilled chicken salad with no dressing, all while I ordered the meatloaf and mashed potatoes.

This newfound humor has transcended to my increased positivity on a whole: I laugh when I think back to when I thought that a breakup and being alone was the worst punishment dealt to anyone, ever. Once I finally relaxed and stopped trying to predict the far-flung future of dating, I simply enjoyed meeting great guys, some of whom I still talk to today, even if we eventually chose not to date.

As Kim smartly advises, even though you have to date to find that perfect mate—dating isn't just about finding your future one and only. If you mistakenly approach it like that, the bar of expectations will be unattainable from the get-go, when the nervous getting-to-know-you conversation is at its most awkward point. I've definitely had to remind myself to recheck my perspective when my expectations were too high. Dating takes time, and it's learning about who you are, and how you react to new personalities. How does another person make you feel? How do you feel around that person? Even though dating can turn into something long-term, you have to begin by approaching it on a short-term basis. Then, after (more) time and whenever you think that you share many of the same outlooks on life, like with career, family, and money choices—well, then that's when you can look at that person and the future of your dating life a little more seriously.

Going forward, like I'm doing now, try to go on dates with the intention that to learn is to laugh. If I can't laugh right now, if I truly can't laugh and appreciate a night out over a stinky plate of meats and cheeses, then how can I expect a wonderful woman like Kim to find humor and, ultimately, peace in life? I want more for myself and for wonderful people like Kim. I want to choose humor over disappointment, and I think that everyone brings their own interesting story and lesson to the table—the good, the bad…

…and even the freaks and the jerks.

12

The Conclusion to My Melodramatic Program

I find that people love lists, especially when you're writing them to dole out advice. Lists are short and sweet and, even if people don't actually identify with anything except for point number 7, then they still think the list applies to them.

Hopefully, though, you can identify with and try your best to follow all points on how to survive and get over your breakup:

1) Cry a lot and stop feeling guilty about it
2) Brush your teeth *every day*
3) Make lists of goals
4) Try to love yourself by figuring out why you love yourself
5) Form routines
6) Stop texting your friends and actually call them

And finally, the most important and last step:

7) Learn to love yourself, and then—get over yourself.

Remember that there will always be more to life: the bad can be worse, but the good that you're not expecting will always turn out to be much, much better. No matter what's thrown at you, be kind. And stay humble.

Finally, put in the work. I've become my own genuine person by bouncing back from a layoff, moving twice before finally getting it right, and paying off my debt. Now, I've rediscovered my love for writing—I've written a book and launched a blog, I freelance, and I recently purchased my first home. I've also learned that the love from a puppy can be exponentially expressed without words. I have reconnected with a lot of friends. I'm finally… happy.

Now, my friend, it's time for you to go do you. It's time to go onwards and upwards, and it's time to start now. I hope you'll share your story with me.

Acknowledgments

The support of my family is abnormally special. Thank you to my mom, dad, brothers, and sister. Thank you for recognizing my calling to write at an early age: the lengthy multiple choice questions for Santa, and the need for school supplies and blank journals in lieu of makeup for my vanity. Thank you for your consistent forward pushes to nurture my talents and for my inherited uncommon work ethic.

Thank you, God, for your guidance; I need to learn to lean on you more.

My friends deserve special recognition. Rachael, you're so special. When I write about you, I cry, and I never cry. You're an incredible mom and human being. Katie, you are everything in a best friend. You listen to my repetitive loops and your selflessness inspires me. Laura, you're like a sister, and I'm so proud of you. Kristen, thank you for our inside jokes and with more to come.

Chris, Amelia, Andrea, Caitlin, and Brian: thanks for your advice, particularly when I needed it the most. Melissa and Derek, thank you for your laughs and artistry.

To the M. family and E.M., thank you for welcoming me and Teddy into your families.

Finally, much gratitude to Kevin and Isabella. I'm humbled that you thought that what I had to say was worth sharing in print.

Thank you, thank you, thank you.

About the Author

Lisa Cleary is a self-help and lifestyle writer—with a focus on interactions, mindsets, and goals. Her work bypasses a cheerleader-type approach, and instead realistically dives into our everyday obstacles and issues, discussing a more authentic way of life.

She contributes to TODAY and Love What Matters, and has contributed to *The Huffington Post* and *Women's Health*. She was a former daily health columnist for *NBC* (DC).

Cleary directs and writes content for her website, www.LisaCleary.com. She features interviews with celebrities, public figures, and business leaders on their perspectives, vulnerabilities and mistakes, and tips for personal improvement. She also writes about herself, uncensored, to help at least one person feel less alone.

How to Survive a Breakup: (When all of your friends are birthing their second child) is her debut title. She is currently working on a second title, as well as a children's book.

Connect with Lisa Cleary at:

www.LisaCleary.com

Instagram @lisacleary3

Twitter @LisaCleary3

Apprentice
House Press
Loyola University Maryland

Apprentice House is the country's only campus-based, student-staffed book publishing company. Directed by professors and industry professionals, it is a nonprofit activity of the Communication Department at Loyola University Maryland.

Using state-of-the-art technology and an experiential learning model of education, Apprentice House publishes books in untraditional ways. This dual responsibility as publishers and educators creates an unprecedented collaborative environment among faculty and students, while teaching tomorrow's editors, designers, and marketers.

Outside of class, progress on book projects is carried forth by the AH Book Publishing Club, a co-curricular campus organization supported by Loyola University Maryland's Office of Student Activities.

Eclectic and provocative, Apprentice House titles intend to entertain as well as spark dialogue on a variety of topics. Financial contributions to sustain the press's work are welcomed. Contributions are tax deductible to the fullest extent allowed by the IRS.

To learn more about Apprentice House books or to obtain submission guidelines, please visit www.apprenticehouse.com.

Apprentice House
Communication Department
Loyola University Maryland
4501 N. Charles Street
Baltimore, MD 21210
Ph: 410-617-5265
info@apprenticehouse.com • www.apprenticehouse.com

9 781627 202657